The Search for Compassion

The Search for Compassion

Spirituality and Ministry

Andrew Purves

Westminster/John Knox Press
Louisville, Kentucky

Book design by Gene Harris

First edition

Published by Westminster/John Knox Press
Louisville, Kentucky

PRINTED IN THE UNITED STATES OF AMERICA

9 8 7 6 5 4 3 2 1

Library of Congress Cataloging-in-Publication Data

Purves, Andrew, 1946–
   The search for compassion : spirituality and ministry / Andrew Purves. — 1st. ed.
      p.   cm.
   ISBN 0-664-25065-3

   1. Clergy—Religious life. 2. Pastoral theology. 3. Sympathy—Religious aspects—Christianity. 4. Suffering—Religious aspects—Christianity. 5. Identification (Religion) 6. Spirituality. I. Title.
BV4011.6.P87 1989
253 '.2—dc20

89-31962
CIP

Contents

Preface

I discovered compassion as I was treated compassionately during personal crises in my own life. My father, an un-schooled man of quiet faith, was my first teacher in compassion through the quality of his unconditional love. My teacher and friend Bill Shaw, now Professor of Theology in the University of St. Andrews in Scotland, supported me through some difficult years and impressed me with his integrity and faith; his compassion became a model of Christian ministry for me. Even closer to home, watching Cathy, my wife, with our children has perhaps taught me more about compassion than she will ever know. Each of us can probably tell similar stories about how we have been touched and shaped by the compassion of others.

In my early thirties, I was a parish minister in rural western Pennsylvania and trying to figure out what ministry was all about. A list of degrees and a tool bag full of pastoral skills somehow did not seem adequate for the task before me. Ministry had to be more than rather stuffy preaching and the application of the contemporary pastoral technologies. Certainly I cared for my congregation, and I knew how to care in a professional way. But something was missing. More than once during these years I wondered and worried about the linchpin of my ministry, what it was that held it all together.

My Scottish theological training had equipped me with a high doctrine of Jesus Christ. I had all the words right, but I lacked an abiding sense of Jesus Christ in my ministry in any real way. I could not get hold of him. In practical terms, Jesus was remote. He kept slipping away from me, crucified again on the cross of a thousand theological abstractions.

Prompted by a colleague, I made a retreat with the Wellspring Mission Group of the Church of the Saviour in Washington, D.C. Two things happened over the four days of the retreat. I discovered for the first time that prayer was possible for me, and Gordon Cosby, pastor of the Church of the Saviour, introduced me to the compassion of Jesus. In one sense I mark these days as the time of my conversion. Nothing would ever be quite the same again. Prayer and compassion came together for me to form the center I sought. Relationship with Jesus and the awareness that I was called through that relationship to participate in his continuing ministry of compassion meant that my ministry, and indeed my sense of the Christian faith, was now being recast.

I quickly discovered that compassion was a neglected concept. I found almost nothing written about it, and few people expressed any sense that it might be important. Matthew Fox's *A Spirituality Named Compassion and the Healing of the Global Village, Humpty Dumpty and Us* was a joy to discover, although as a liberal Roman Catholic he represented a theological tradition far different from my own. Later on, Donald P. McNeill, Douglas A. Morrison, and Henri J. M. Nouwen published *Compassion: A Reflection on the Christian Life.* It is hard to overemphasize the beauty and pathos of this little volume. But neither book really attempted to wrestle with theological and pastoral concerns. What was the nature of Jesus' compassion? Can we speak sensibly of the compassion of God? How can I become a compassionate person in ministry?

I explored the area mapped out by my discovery of prayer and compassion, trying to hold them together, trying to understand their mysteries, trying to get a sense of what they meant for my life, faith, and ministry. These initial searchings led me to a conclusion that has never

wavered: We study compassion in order to find out something of what went on at the center of Jesus' life and
ministry; we pray so that we can grow in relationship with
Jesus and participate thereby in his continuing compassion.

A number of persons contributed to this study in various
ways. The support of the Board of Directors and President
C. Samuel Calian of Pittsburgh Theological Seminary in
granting me a sabbatical leave to complete the work, I
recognize with thankfulness. Dean Ulrich Mauser has
been a nurturing colleague and friend who believed in this
project from the beginning. Needless to say, many students have been on the receiving end of this material. The
joy with which at least a few of them considered my reflections was a constant support. Many clergy and congre-
gations in western Pennsylvania and Ohio heard bits and
pieces of this material at various stages of production.
Their sense that I was writing something for the church
encouraged me enormously. Pat Nelson, a student at Pittsburgh Theological Seminary, read the manuscript with
great care, and I am grateful to her for that. My gratitude
to Cathy and our children, Brendan, Gordon, and Laura,
cannot be reduced to a few words. They let me get on with
it, put up with the emotional ups and downs of writing,
and helped me to keep the whole thing in perspective.
Cathy also read and commented on the text, and it is
significantly more readable as a result. Needless to say, all
errors and confusions are mine alone.

I dedicate this book with love to my late father, Jimmy
Purves. As I said, he was my first teacher in compassion.

Introduction: The Search for a Renewed Compassion

No day is an ordinary day. But on one day recently I began reading Nicholas Wolterstorff's book *Lament for a Son*, a staggeringly vulnerable account of grief and intense theological and spiritual questioning over the death of his son in a climbing accident at the age of twenty-five. On that same day, a former student told me of her mother's imminent death from cancer. A colleague telephoned to cancel a retreat I was to lead for his staff the next day because his organist's mother had hanged herself. I read on that day of the prospects of further drought in Africa. And I discovered I had influenza.

Life is hard. Certainly there is more to life than suffering, but suffering is inevitably part of the story. The case for our exposure to suffering hardly needs to be made.

It is evident that what we and everyone else in the world need in our suffering and sorrow are people who will care for us. It may not be the only thing we all need, but it is always a part of what is needed. Wolterstorff, in his book, remarks:

> But please: Don't say it's not really so bad. Because it is. Death is awful, demonic. If you think your task as comforter is to tell me that really, all things considered, it's not so bad, you do not sit with me in my grief but place yourself off in the distance away from me. What I need to hear from you is that you recognize how painful it is. I need to hear from you that you are with

me in my desperation. To comfort me, you have to
come close. Come sit beside me on my mourning
bench.[1]

Wolterstorff's plea is for a renewed compassion.

How is a renewed compassion possible for us? It is probably a matter of time before the intensity of suffering in
others leads us to harden our hearts against it. After all,
there is only so much suffering any of us can take before
we are simply overwhelmed by it. We can only sit on the
mourning bench for a while. We who would suffer with
others can become casualties of the very acts of our love.
Our compassion recoils, as it were, making us its victims.
We begin to realize, perhaps, that exposure to too much
suffering will destroy us as well. It will drive us mad. And
so we shut off, or at least very carefully control, our sensitivity to the suffering of others, often being unaware that
we are doing so.

We need a Christian pastoral spirituality that is able to
answer the concerns we feel about being faithful in ministry today. It is the purpose of this study on compassion to
address that need head-on. In the first place, compassion,
as we will discover, is deeply rooted in the life of God
revealed to us in Jesus of Nazareth. Compassion reveals
the inner nature of God. That which we need in our suffering—namely, a sense of having a companion beside us
on the mourning bench—is what we find God to be for us
in Jesus of Nazareth. In the second place, compassion is
only possible for us in and through our relationship with
God in Christ. Compassionate living is the result of that
relationship. Through our relationship with God in Jesus
Christ we inevitably participate in God's continuing compassion for the world. Compassion, in other words, does
not call for an abstracted, free-floating spirituality, and it
certainly does not impose an impossible moral imperative.
It is a way of living in Christ and through Christ in ministry
to the suffering of the world. Theology, spirituality, and
ministry become the threads of an emerging tapestry of
faith and life.

It is not yet clear, however, that the church is equipped to meet the pastoral challenge of the years ahead. On the one hand, spirituality remains today a distant reality for many Christians, especially Protestant Christians. On the other hand, there is profound confusion over the nature of ministry.

A renewed compassion will only be possible because of a renewed spirituality. A renewed spirituality will be a spirituality of Christian maturity in which we are so formed by Jesus Christ that we are transformed by him and come more and more to share his nature.[2] This renewed spirituality in which we grow up in every way into Christ, who is the head (Eph. 4:15), is a process that proceeds through the expected disciplines of the Christian life: prayer, the reading of the Bible, worship. But the goal is not piety. Rather, a renewed spirituality will be a process of confrontation, exploration, and struggle with those parts of ourselves that remain resistant to the claims of Christ and his ministry.

The nature of ministry is difficult to pin down. The ministry of the laity, for example, is in thralldom to a spirit of volunteerism. Therefore, ministry is understood to be what one does in one's spare time. Volunteerism in ministry really means that authorities other than God have staked a prior claim on one's allegiance. This leads inevitably to the privatization of Christianity, because faith is pushed to the margins of public life.

The ministry of the clergy is in a state of deep and damaging confusion. What is a clergyperson supposed to do? He or she is a worship leader and a preacher, a teacher, a student and theologian, an administrator, a program director, a pastor and, if possible, a pastoral counselor, a community organizer, and perhaps even the person who fixes the boiler and turns off the lights at the end of the day. He or she should also be a paragon of virtue, constant in prayer and study. Increasingly, members of the clergy feel that they are the Jack or Jill of all trades and the master or mistress of none. They are often very poorly paid, certainly feel that they are not shown much real respect, and they may well be conspicuously overworking and in a quandary over what to do about it. In the face of all of this, many clergy today suffer from a plummeting sense of personal self-respect and an acute loss of professional identity and satisfaction. We have here, I believe, a crisis before the church of quite mammoth proportions, a crisis that is at once theological, spiritual, and professional.

The study of compassion will not solve all the concerns raised here. But it is valid to claim that the search for a renewed compassion is certainly one starting place where both laity and clergy can acquire a profound sense of rootedness in the life of God and can experience the liberating and energizing connection between this rootedness, this spirituality, and ministry. It is this connection between spirituality and ministry, at once both dynamic and particular, which gives ministry its power, its identity, and its direction. Ministry becomes an expression then of life in God and of God's care for the world. Compassion functions not simply as a metaphor for ministry, giving ministry shape and content, but as a source of ministry that grows out of the life of God and of God's care for the world.

It should be clear by now that compassion has a special meaning, although it may not yet be clear what that meaning is. I begin my classes on compassion with a simple exercise. I invite the students to define the term. The definitions usually include commonly perceived synonyms like sympathy, empathy, pity, mercy, love, care, concern, and the feeling of sorrow for another. As we work through the list, the students begin to express a hint of recognition that maybe they have not yet defined compassion adequately. There is something more to discover.

Henri Nouwen has said somewhere that the English word "care" can be traced back to an old Gothic word *Kara*, which means "to lament, to weep with, to grieve." Caring, in other words, has to do with deep feelings that arise within us as we move into relationships with those who suffer. This understanding is very close to what we mean by compassion. The English word "compassion" is

derived from two Latin words, *com* and *pati,* which together mean "to bear with" or "to suffer with." At the
common level of use, then, compassion is understood to be
a sympathetic awareness of another's distress, with a desire to alleviate it in some way. But we must turn to our
theological heritage if we are to understand the deeper
meaning.

Compassion has a profound theological meaning. This
book is an inquiry into that meaning and its significance
for Christian life and ministry as they are revealed to us
in God's history with Israel and in the ministry and teaching of Jesus of Nazareth. While in common usage compassion may have an agreeable but slightly ineffective sense
to it, in the New Testament especially it is found to be a
theological word of considerable power and particularity.
A case can be made for seeing compassion as the center
of pastoral care. Compassion makes caring specific. Compassion radicalizes caring, giving our caring root in the
deepest places of God's being.

Biblically, compassion is an action word that does more
than describe an admirable emotional state. In the Gospels
compassion is a verb, a "remarkable verb," as Karl Barth
calls it.[3] Our English language cannot express this subtle
yet theologically important verbal dimension of compassion. In English we either act with compassion or we are
compassionate. We are unable to say that we "compassion" someone. Something of the dynamism of compassion
is thereby lost in translation. The New Testament, on the
other hand, intends compassion to have a meaning somewhere between acting with compassion and being compassionate. It steers a course between the action-oriented
noun and the interior and slightly passive sense of the
adjective. It includes both, yet suggests a synthesis in
which the outward ministry of compassion and the inner
quality of one's affections belong together in the one
movement.

"Compassion" is also a technical theological word. It was
used in the Bible to characterize God's self-revelation to
Israel, and it shaped the life of the community called out

by that revelation. In the New Testament, the verb is used only of Jesus or by Jesus to refer to figures in parables who represent God or himself. It has messianic or christological particularity. Now this is a terribly important point. Because Jesus was wholly God and wholly a human person, Jesus' compassion tells us something unique about who God is and how God relates to us. Jesus' compassion becomes a window of access into the nature of God and God's way of being in ministry toward us. God's compassion requires us to understand God now in terms of God's vulnerability and willingness to suffer with us. This calls for a revolution in our concept of God in which we no longer understand God to be an unchangeable, unaffected being who loves us in distant untouchability. Instead, we discover God to be the one who knows suffering intimately and who is changed by that experience.

The study of compassion takes us beyond the familiar sense of the word. In fact, the study of compassion takes us into new theological territory with respect to our understanding of God, ministry, and the spiritual life. The search for a renewed compassion becomes an exercise in pastoral theology, which is the inquiry into the meaning and significance of the gospel for the ministry and life of the church.

The vision that lies at the heart of this book is the belief that our ministries of compassion arise out of our relationship with Jesus Christ, who alone is the compassionate one. Theological identity, spiritual maturity, and ministry grounded in the life and will of God belong together. Our compassion is a participation in Jesus' compassion. We who have our identity "in Christ," as the apostle Paul puts it, will discover that compassion is the gift and demand of grace.

1

"And he had compassion on them": Compassion in the Ministry of Jesus

The practice of compassion is the practice of ministry. Compassion means ministry. It is not simply sympathy or the expression of well-meaning good intention. Compassion means getting involved in another's life for healing and wholeness. The logic of compassion moves from a deep feeling for another who is suffering to a ministering work of some kind. In every instance where Jesus is reported to have had compassion, it is also reported that he engaged in a subsequent act of ministry.

There is a *Peanuts* cartoon in which Charlie Brown approaches one of his friends and asks her if she is concerned about world hunger. She shrugs her shoulders in implied indifference to the issue. Charlie Brown approaches a second and then a third friend and poses the same question. In each case he receives the same reply of implied indifference. Finally Charlie Brown explodes in righteous indignation: "Well, at least I feel guilty about it."[1] Although Charlie Brown has a heart deeply moved over the plight of the hungry, unfortunately he does not have compassion on them. He has sympathy, or something like it. The point is: Compassion always leads to acts of ministry in which the situation is addressed in some way for healing or wholeness.

The verb "to have compassion"—*splanchnizomai* in the Greek New Testament—is used nine times in reference to Jesus in the Gospels (including the disputed text at Mark 1:41). Compassion is also found at Mark 6:34, 8:2, and 9:22; at Matthew 9:36, 14:14, 15:32, and 20:34, and at Luke 7:13. Further, Jesus used compassion as a verb in three parables, at Matthew 18:27 and at Luke 10:33 and 15:20.[2]

Compassion in the New Testament literally means to have one's bowels turned over. The word refers to what we would perhaps call a "gut-wrenching" experience. *Splanchnizomai*, compassion, this rather unusual New Testament verb, refers to a feeling of solidarity with another that is virtually physical in its effect. There is nothing genteel or comely about compassion.

In this first chapter we will explore compassion in the ministry of Jesus. We will examine each recorded instance, allowing the texts to guide us toward a deeper understanding of compassion. As appropriate, we will move from discussion of the texts to theological and pastoral reflection. In this way we should begin to see more and more clearly and precisely what compassion is in the New Testament and what it involves for Christian life. Chapter 2 will pursue a similar course with respect to compassion in the teaching of Jesus in the parables.

The Healing of the Leper (Mark 1:40–45)

This deceptively simple healing story ably illustrates the primary point: Compassion means ministry. A leper approached Jesus and begged to be healed. The leper had faith that if Jesus desired to heal him, he would be healed. In compassion,[3] Jesus touched the leper and commanded him to be free of the disease. Immediately he was healed. Jesus then dismissed the leper with the strict instruction to say nothing about the healing and to attend at once to the ceremonial religious purification rites, the completion of which would allow him to have free access to social relations again. The healed leper, however, for whatever reason, did not do as Jesus required of him. Instead, he spread the story of his healing far and wide. This apparently caused such an interest that Jesus could no longer show himself in the towns.

In biblical times lepers led truly awful lives. Leprosy was not only a loathsome and disfiguring skin disease, its physical aspect was compounded by emotional and social suffering. By religious law the leper was cast out from the community. "He shall remain unclean as long as he has the disease; he is unclean; he shall dwell alone in a habitation outside the camp" (Lev. 13:46). The leper was required to broadcast his or her state by wearing torn clothing, by having wild hair, by covering his upper lip, and by shouting "Unclean! Unclean!" Sometimes a bell was worn around the leper's neck to warn others of his or her approach. An expeditious retreat was expected. Lepers, in other words, were excommunicated from society. They were marginalized, pushed to the edge, and treated as less than human in order to protect the rest of society from infection.

While leprosy is almost eradicated in our day, other diseases or conditions have taken its place, carrying with them a similar degree of physical, emotional, and social suffering. Some persons with AIDS, for example, experience life in a way similar to the leper in biblical times. The men, women, and children who live on the streets of our large cities, sometimes suffering acute mental illness, are invariably treated as lepers. The unfortunate and distasteful image of the "social leper" comes to mind here, an image used by some observers to describe those persons who they believe are parasites on society. Whatever the merits or demerits of various political prescriptions, to treat another person as a leper, for whatever reason, is to treat that person with callous disdain and inhumaneness. It is to cast the person beyond the pale of human community. Perhaps, too, the way in which many older persons are abandoned by relatives and friends suggests a marginalization akin to leprosy.

Jesus broke religious and social regulations simply by remaining where he was. Before he lifted a hand to help

the leper, Jesus had already demonstrated a basic humanity. He allowed himself to be in relationship with a person
who was to be treated as "outside the gate." By not obeying the regulations Jesus not only put himself beyond the
pale, becoming himself unclean, but also ran the risk
surely of contracting the disease. In all, just by holding his
ground, Jesus demonstrated a depth of purpose and concern for the leper.

Mark 1:41 states that Jesus was moved with compassion.
(The RSV use of "pity" is inaccurate. *Splanchnizomai* is
properly translated "have compassion.") Clearly Jesus had
to have been very deeply moved to have acted as he did.
Compassion is not a superficial emotion. He was moved in
his inner depths over the leper's awful plight. He was
moved toward relationship and healing.

Jesus touched the leper. The enormity of that act is
probably lost on us today. William Lane, in his commentary on Mark, remarks that

> the touch of Jesus was significant from two points of
> view. From the perspective of the leper it was an act
> of unheard-of compassion which must have moved him
> deeply and strengthened him in his conviction he had
> not asked for help in vain. From the perspective of
> Jesus' relationship to the cultic and ritual system, it
> indicated that he did not hesitate to act in violation of
> its regulations when the situation demanded.[4]

At the touch, the leper was healed.

Compassion and touch often go together. Indeed, we
might put it colloquially: Compassion is a hands-on ministry. Of the compassion texts, the following also involve
touch: the healing of the epileptic youth at Mark 9:14–29;
the cure of the two blind men at Matthew 20:29–34; the
raising of the dead son of the widow of Nain at Luke
7:11–17. Two of the parables of compassion also illustrate
the connection between compassion and touch: the father
embraced the returning prodigal son (Luke 15:20) and the
good Samaritan poured oil on and bound the wounds of
the injured traveler (Luke 10:34). Compassion is a touch-

ing ministry, a ministry in which one is physically involved with the other.

The hands-on quality of compassion need not surprise us. Touching has long had a place in the Christian pastoral tradition as a vehicle of blessing and healing. Hands are laid on sick persons. The sick may also be anointed with oil (James 5:14). God's blessing is given through the laying of hands upon the head. In some traditions that is ritually enacted when, at the close of the service of worship, the minister's hands are raised as the benediction is pronounced over the people. The action symbolizes the laying of hands upon the head of every person present. The kiss of peace, the hug, and the formal handshake in greeting also illustrate how touch has a place in religious life. Touch is a means of grace.

The connection between compassion and touch makes concrete something of the inner logic of compassion that was recognized by Thomas Merton. Merton was a twentieth-century American monk. In an address delivered in Bangkok on the day of his tragic early death he said that "the whole idea of compassion . . . is based on a keen awareness of the interdependence of all these living beings, which are all part of one another and all involved in one another."[5] Jesus' response to the leper was in no small way the recognition of interdependency and interrelatedness. In his action, Jesus affirmed that he and the leper belonged together.

In this story of the healing of the leper we catch a glimpse of divine compassion. In Jesus' compassion the inner heart and hurt of God are laid open before us. We get a hint here of the extent to which God in Christ went in order to live truly a self-emptied life for our healing and salvation.

The Healing of the Epileptic Youth (Mark 9:14–29)

This harrowing story has interest not only for its further illumination of compassion but also for its juxtaposition of intense mystical experience, the place of prayer in ministry, desperate human need, a parent called into vicarious faith, and the failure of the disciples to perform a healing miracle. This is a story with many levels, of which compassion is only one.

In Mark's vivid and detailed account, the return of Jesus from the Mount of Transfiguration is marked by a plunge into stark, stubborn, and distressing reality. Spiritually speaking, the mountaintop and the valley are never that far separated. A group had gathered around the disciples and were debating in earnest. Seeing Jesus, they were filled with awe and welcomed him. Upon inquiry, Jesus was told by an anxious and no doubt harried father that he had brought his son to be healed. The father described his son's seizures in clinical detail. The disciples, however, had been unable to heal him. Jesus' weary and exasperated response was a prelude to the command to have the youth brought before him. One senses perhaps that Jesus was near the end of his tether. Immediately the boy went into a seizure in front of Jesus. "How long has he had this?" Jesus asked (v. 21). The father's response was heavy with suffering for his son's sickness: "From childhood. And it has often cast him into the fire and into the water, to destroy him" (v. 22). Then the father pleaded with Jesus: "But if you can do anything, have pity on us and help us" (v. 22). (The translation given by the RSV is inappropriate at this point. The father asked for compassion, not pity, from Jesus.) The father required that Jesus move from sympathy to compassion.

What happened next does not immediately make sense. Instead of healing the youth there and then, as one might have expected, Jesus conducted a catechetical exercise. Seizing upon the father's words just where doubt crept in, Jesus demanded faith from the father. The father's response is well known: "I believe; help my unbelief!" As the crowd closed in on Jesus, he uttered the words of healing command. The youth again went into a seizure, such that it looked as though he were dead. Jesus then took him by the hand, raised him to his feet, and he stood.

The story ends with a fascinating vignette between

Jesus and his disciples. They asked why they had been unable to perform the miracle. Jesus' cryptic response points right to the heart of ministry: This kind of miracle is possible only by the power of prayer.

Two issues concern us: the delay in healing the youth, because of Jesus' questioning of the father, and the relationship between compassionate ministry and prayer.

At first glance, it appears that Jesus would have acted more compassionately[6] had he healed the youth, who was in mid-seizure, before dealing with the question of the father's faith. Was Jesus more concerned about right belief than with addressing extreme human need?

There is no obvious answer. But borrowing from our present understanding of the ways in which the members of families and groups interact, it seems plausible to suggest that Mark's account makes good sense when we hold together the father's struggle for faith and the boy's illness. The father's faith and the boy's healing cannot be separated. They are one system. We can only guess at what the specific connection between the father's faith and the son's healing might have been. Nevertheless, it seems reasonable to argue that Jesus acted on the basis of some such connection. To suggest otherwise would be to charge Jesus with Phariseeism, with concern for ritual correctness over true concern for another's plight.

We all have a part to play in our own healing. This is what the father perhaps had to come to recognize. And vicariously, he had a part to play in his son's healing, and that part involved, in some way unknown to us, his faith in God. Carrying forward the image of the family as one organic system, the father's coming to faith and the boy's healing were tied up together. Is it not possible that Jesus recognized this and dealt with it, thereby healing both father and son? Further, is it not possible that the disciples did not discern the symbiotic relationship between the father's lack of faith and the son's illness, and so could not heal the son? If this interpretation is correct, we can say that Jesus' compassion drove much more deeply into the plight of the father and son than either the father or the disciples believed was necessary. Not a bandage but radical surgery was required.

Compassion does not allow the recipient to remain passive. It does not induce quietism. In compassion, Jesus does not act as a magician or wonder-worker. In this story he required the father to do from his side what was necessary for the healing to be successful. In other words, the issue is precisely that of cheap or costly grace. Dietrich Bonhoeffer's words provide a suitable commentary on this aspect of compassion.

> Cheap grace is the preaching of forgiveness without requiring repentance, baptism without church discipline, Communion without confession, absolution without personal confession. Cheap grace is grace without discipline, grace without the cross, grace without Jesus Christ, living and incarnate. . . . Costly grace is the gospel which must be *sought* again and again, the gift which must be *asked* for, the door at which a man must *knock*. Such grace is *costly* because it calls us to follow, and it is *grace* because it calls us to follow *Jesus Christ.*[7]

Compassionate ministry, if it is not to be cheap grace, must, when necessary and appropriate, call forth responsibility from the sufferer. In this sense it is an evangelical ministry. It is not paternalism, a superior kind of do-goodism, which does things *for* people rather than *with* them. It treats people as responsible adults who more than likely have a role to play in their healing and wholeness.

The second issue this story suggests for us is the relationship between compassion and prayer. Jesus' brief conversation with the disciples at Mark 9:28–29 is enigmatic, leaving us with the hint of a solution to the disciples' failure to perform the miracle. Jesus' discernment of the problem with the youth apparently was the result of profound spiritual insight. The footnote to this text tells us that some manuscripts also add fasting to prayer. This means that a regime of rigorous spiritual discipline was necessary for the full ministry of compassion to come to pass. In other words, compassion is not a skill to be learned, or a program to be administered, or a technique to be applied. There can be no officially accredited compassionate persons. Compassion is a ministry, rather, which arises out of deep relationship with God. This is a critical issue in the study of compassion. We raise it now because it arises out of the passage. Its full treatment, however, must wait until a later chapter, when we have a clearer and fuller sense of the meaning of compassion.

The Feeding Stories (Mark 6:30–44; 8:1–10; and pars.)

A host of issues and problems surround the feeding stories in the Gospels. Was there one feeding incident, reported in two independent traditions? Or were there in fact two separate incidents? What are we to make of the differences and similarities in the accounts? What was the nature of the miracles? Where did they occur and with what group of people? What meaning do the feeding stories have for our lives of faith today? What relation do the feeding stories have to our understanding of the Lord's Supper? It is not our purpose here to address every problem raised by the study of these stories. Our purpose rather is to understand the accounts adequately insofar as they help us to come to deeper knowledge of the compassion which Jesus had for the crowd.

We will begin with the first feeding story in Mark. It moves from an elaborate twofold introduction (6:30–34), through an extended dialogue with the disciples (6:35–38), to the actual feeding event (6:39–44).[8] It is at verse 34 where we read that Jesus had compassion on the crowd, because they were like sheep without a shepherd.

At the conclusion of their mission—today we would probably call it field education!—to the Galilean villages, the disciples returned to Jesus to report on their work and experience. Apparently the disciples had made an impact with their work among the people. We are told that a large number of people were crowding in upon them. It may be that they were even organized in relays ("many were coming and going," v. 31). They could not gather with Jesus in peace. Jesus, sensitive to the disciples' need for rest and debriefing, suggested that they retreat by boat to a lonely place, away from the crowd. There is the idea here of well-deserved rest after strenuous labor. But more, the wilderness motif contains the powerful and evocative sense of the disciples' depleted spiritual condition. They also needed to be ministered to by Jesus. In other words, the disciples were physically and spiritually exhausted.[9]

The crowd, however, was not to be denied. They ran ahead to where Jesus and his party would disembark. Jesus, as he stepped out of the boat, had compassion on the crowd because they were like sheep without a shepherd, and he had much that he wanted to teach them. Luke notes that he taught them about the kingdom of God and cured their sick (Luke 9:11).

Jesus again was very deeply moved, so much so that he canceled his already firm resolve to spend time alone with his disciples. Compassion caused Jesus to rearrange his priorities. The immediate focus of Jesus' compassion was the crowd. It is worth noting that compassion is not restricted to one-to-one relationships. Compassion includes social as well as pastoral ministry, ministry to large numbers of persons as well as ministry to individuals.

It is important to look now at Mark's characterization of the crowd as sheep without a shepherd. The allusion is to Numbers 27:17 and Ezekiel 34:5. Ulrich Mauser comments that, "while the shepherd motif occurs in various different meanings in the Old Testament, it must be noticed that in the context of both passages mentioned it belongs to the wilderness theme."[10] This theme implies both the need of the crowd for guidance and their dependence upon God for deliverance.

At Numbers 27:17, Moses, who is soon to die, asks God to appoint a leader in his place so that the people will not be like sheep without a shepherd. Ezekiel 34 discusses at length the shepherds, or pastors, of Israel, and again shepherding of the people is tied to the wilderness motif. Not only is the faithlessness of the shepherds or pastors of the people decried, and the plight of the people described in terms of divine anguish, but also the announcement is made of the coming of a faithful shepherd who will not abandon the sheep. "Jesus is seen in Mark 6:34 on the background of these passages," comments Mauser.[11] Jesus is the one appointed by God to be the leader of the people in their exodus through the wilderness. He is God's Davidic servant, who will give the people wilderness rest. Mauser's discussion of Mark 6:34, which is the prelude to the feeding and the focus of Jesus' compassion, demonstrates that this passage is making a significant theological statement.

The people are seen by Jesus as if in the wilderness. It is this which evokes his compassion. The need is twofold: for food, a need which is met by the feeding miracle, and for spiritual direction and nurture. It is the spiritual need that is given priority by Mark and is the immediate focus of Jesus' compassion. Mark simply notes that Jesus had much to teach them. Interestingly, in the parallel passage at Matthew 14:14, the immediate need was for healing. Taking the parallel texts together, we can see that compassion is not a ministry exclusively to spiritual needs or to physical needs or to sickness of one kind or another. Different situations suggest different priorities. Compassion clearly is a ministry to the whole person, although usually only under one or two aspects at any one time.

The combination of teaching and feeding is a biblical sign of the breaking in of the new age of God's peace. Incarnate in Jesus Christ, the future rest of the kingdom of God is now present among the people. Mark simply has Jesus enact what Luke names as the content: namely, the kingdom of God. Compassion, then, is here related in Mark to the most profound human need for hope, which Jesus Christ alone can fulfill. Seen in this light we can understand why Jesus rearranged his priorities as far as the weary disciples were concerned. In a subtle and hidden way, the story of the feeding of the five thousand in Mark is the gospel in a nutshell.

The climax of the story is the actual miraculous event of

feeding a large number of people out of extremely meager resources. The immediate prelude to the feeding is the dialogue between Jesus and the disciples about the crowd and their need. Of special interest is the fact that in Mark the food had to be provided by the disciples. It is as though in saying, "You give them something to eat," Jesus is really saying, "You too show them compassion." That the disciples were baffled by this may allow us to suggest that just as the disciples had to be patiently taught the mysteries of the kingdom of God, so too the ways of compassion had to be learned. In order to be compassionate they would have to rely on the power of God's compassion. The disciples could not engage in a ministry of compassion if it were grounded in the shallow soil of their own spiritual strength. A compassionate ministry must be grounded in God and God's own compassion for the world. This the disciples had to discover for themselves.

At the command of Jesus the crowd sat down in groups. A blessing was offered by Jesus, who was the host. The five loaves and two fish were distributed to the people, and all ate their fill. Scraps to fill twelve baskets were later collected. In all, says Mark, five thousand men were fed that day.

William Lane remarks in his discussion of this passage that "the ground of Jesus' compassion is that the people are like sheep who possess no shepherd. Jesus provides the leadership they lack by *teaching them.* The relationship established in the text is between compassion and teaching, while the feeding of the multitude is a subsequent act."[12] That, in summary form, is the significance of the first feeding story in Mark.

The parallel story at Matthew 14:14–21 is different in a number of points of detail.[13] As far as we are concerned, the significant difference is the way in which compassion is expressed in the two accounts. In Mark, Jesus' compassion led him to teach and then to feed. In Matthew, Jesus is moved by his compassion to heal and then to feed the crowd.

Four out of the nine Gospel accounts of Jesus' compassion deal with specific healing miracles: Mark 1:40–45, 9:14–29; Matthew 20:29–34; and Luke 7:11–17, assuming that the raising of the widow's son can be spoken of in this way. And here, at Matthew 14:14, the general linking of compassion and healing is established.

What does this connection mean for us today? How does it challenge us? First of all, we recognize that, according to contemporary wisdom, efficient medicine proceeds on the basis of clinical detachment to some extent at least. Medicine is science as well as art. We surely expect the physician to care for the patient, but in such a way that his or her feelings for the patient do not confound skillful medical judgment. There is good healing sense in the prevailing orthodoxy of necessary clinical detachment. Medicine as a science is simply astonishing in its clinical capacity. People today live longer, healthier lives. Yet when the subtle balance between compassion and healing is forgotten, patients frequently complain of being treated like impersonal objects, or slabs of meat, or "the gallbladder down the hall." In an aggressive clinical scientific environment it may be possible to forget that there is more to health than a well-functioning body and more to healing than clinical efficiency.

The evangelists made a careful connection between compassion and healing. Compassion, which is surely possible in contemporary medicine, must coexist in a carefully nurtured relationship with scientific and therapeutic requirements. But this relationship between compassion and medicine seems to be very subtle and difficult to discern and maintain, given the aggressive scientific orientation of modern medicine and the neglect of the study of compassion in pastoral theology today. It is encouraging to discover physicians and theologians who are concerned about compassionate medicine and who have taken up the challenge to explore the shape and content of that elusive relationship.

Secondly, we recognize that healing has become the province of a highly specialized and controlled medical guild. The church's involvement in health and healing have declined markedly as health, along with education and social welfare, has been handed over to state or private enterprises regarded as better equipped to render efficient service.

The biblical connection between compassion and healing invites us to question the declining role of the church in the healing process. Again, the issues are subtle and complex. On the one hand, nonmedical persons feel understandably intimidated by contemporary medicine. On the other hand, Christians do have to face the theological questions involved in the virtual abdication of the church from healing. Are the traditional healing ministries of the church—anointing with oil, prayer and the laying on of hands, Eucharist for the sick, and the admonition and comfort of the word—obsolete today in the face of modern medicine?

At the very least, compassion involves companionship with the sick: "I was sick and you visited me" (Matt. 25:36). But more must be said. I have the strongest sense that Christians who are sick, or in any kind of distress, want the ministry of the church, the ministry of the word. Yet few clergy are trained today to see pastoral care as a ministry of the word. When pastoral care is collapsed into pastoral counseling at the expense of the pastoral ministry of the word, then the church has abandoned its evangelical heritage and commission. As Eugene H. Peterson notes, it is the task of pastoral care to represent the eternal word of God in the ordinary places of life.[14] The recovery of the historical pastoral wisdom of the faith is clearly an issue with which pastors (ministers of the word!), churches, and seminaries have to wrestle.

Further, Christians have a traditional understanding of health as wholeness, and wholeness includes a right relationship with God and with one's fellows. Health is a relational and a spiritual reality as well as a biological and a psychological reality. In other words, Christians called to a ministry of compassion must be involved in the fight for a holistic, integrative understanding of health and for the caring adequacy of health care delivery systems.

Returning now to Matthew's account, we find that the narrative moves directly from the healing to the actual feeding of the crowd. As in Mark, the disciples were confused. Jesus again had to take the initiative. And much food was gathered from the scraps.

As we turn to the second feeding account at Mark 8:1–10 and Matthew 15:32–39, we note again the debate over the legitimacy of this as a separate event. The prevailing scholarly opinion is that we have one event reported twice.[15] The details of this debate need not concern us. There are a number of observations we can make, however, which assist our inquiry into Jesus' compassion.

To begin with, there is a significant difference in the immediate focus of Jesus' compassion in the second two accounts given by Mark and Matthew. In Mark's first account, the movement went from compassion to teaching to feeding. In the second, the movement goes from compassion directly to feeding. The people have been with Jesus for three days and have no food. The supplies have run out. Something must be done. We find the same shift of emphasis in the second account in Matthew. Where before Jesus' compassion led to healing and then to feeding, here it leads directly to feeding.

It is important to highlight the direct emphasis upon feeding. Up to this point we have dealt with feeding only in passing. Now it has center stage. It would be a mistake to assume that compassion only had a role to play in interpersonal ministry, or in ministry to spiritual need and illness. As we find again and again in the Gospels, Jesus was profoundly influenced by the prophets of Israel. Their concern for the poor, for issues of justice and peace, were his concern too. Jesus' ministry was not solely "pastoral," meaning by this a ministry unconcerned with issues of social justice. The study of compassion shows us once and for all that we cannot separate personal and social, spiritual and material concerns, as if persons and ministry to them could be broken up into bits and pieces. Although the connections between pastoral and social ministry are not always self-evident, we are well advised to keep both

in sight, for they are two parts of the one ministry of
compassion which was incarnate in Jesus Christ.

The feeding stories, when taken together, link compassion directly with teaching, healing, and feeding. Compassion leads to multifaceted ministry. Like love, compassion
will lead one along many different paths. It may well lead
beyond conventional responses (and this will be discussed
in the next chapter). One cannot write a rule book for
compassion. There is no one right compassionate response, a response appropriate for all situations. There is
no compassionate equivalent to Robert's *Rules of Order.*

Each account of Jesus' compassion shows him respond-
ing to specific needs in specific ways, as the situation demands. For example, in the account of the healing of the
epileptic youth at Mark 9:14–29 a statement of faith was
elicited from the father, but no such requirement was
made of the widow of Nain, whose son Jesus raised from
the dead. This is all the more noteworthy in view of the
preceding story, at Luke 7:1–10. There Jesus healed the
centurion's servant. The story illustrates exemplary faith.
Or consider again the healing of the leper at Mark 1:40–
45. That healing is set in the context of meeting the Mosaic
regulations, though nowhere else is Jesus' act of compassion tied to the requirements of the religious law.

Pastoral theologian Seward Hiltner has written of what
he called the "good Samaritan principle."[16] By this he
meant to suggest that the ministry of the Samaritan was a
response to the immediate need: that is, he brought the
help which was appropriate to the situation. At another
time and place, when the situation was different, that
same Samaritan might have offered quite a different kind
of assistance, which would have been every bit as compassionate and appropriate. Compassion, in other words, is an
orientation, an availability, a way of life, in which we allow
situations of need to stake their claim upon us in their
uniqueness. It is not a package of preconditioned responses. Compassion is person- and need-specific; it is a
situational ministry. Compassion implies a freedom for
ministry through openness to others in their suffering.

The Healing of the Two Blind Men
(Matthew 20:29–34)

This brief but complex healing story is a provocative commentary on the unsettling conversations that immediately preceded it. These conversations provide a context for Matthew's setting of the healing of the two blind men. In the movement from conversation to healing miracle we see juxtaposed false and true discipleship, discipleship that is self-serving and discipleship that is compassionate.

Jesus and his company were journeying toward Jerusalem. The climax of Jesus' ministry was approaching, and he was teaching his disciples about the stark consequences of his life. Along the way, the mother of James and John, the sons of Zebedee, approached Jesus and implored him to grant places of favor for them. Apparently, the two brothers had rather ungraciously prevailed upon their mother to speak on their behalf, for Jesus in response turned to them and instructed them in the facts of life for those who would follow him. Clearly, the brothers had not yet understood the inner nature of Jesus' ministry or the nature of his claim upon them.

Human nature marks the response of the other disciples; they are indignant. Jesus claims the moment to teach his group the realities of the spiritual life: Whoever wants to be great must be your servant, and whoever wants to be first must be the willing slave of all (Matt. 20:26–27). And now, to drive the message home, at least as we find it in Matthew's presentation, the miracle of the healing of the two blind men follows.

The band were making their way from Jericho to Jerusalem, and a large crowd followed. Two blind men sitting by the roadside heard that Jesus was passing by (compare with Mark 10:46–52 and Luke 18:35–43, the parallel passages, in which only one blind man is healed). They cried out for Jesus to have mercy upon them (v. 30). The request was for a breaking in of divine faithfulness into the dire misery of the human situation. It was a profoundly sophisticated theological request. The attempt by the crowd to silence these importuning blind men only succeeded in stimulating them to greater efforts to be heard by Jesus.

In Matthew's account, Jesus himself called the blind men to come over to him. "What do you want me to do for you?" (v. 32). Their reply states the obvious: "Lord, let our eyes be opened" (v. 33). The account then states that Jesus had compassion upon the men. (The RSV use of "pity" is inaccurate. *Splanchnizonai* is properly translated "compassion.") Their plight touched him deeply, causing him in some way to feel their pain within himself. Jesus was affected, and he was prompted into miraculous healing action. He touched their eyes—again we note the connection between compassion and touch—and the men were healed of their blindness and followed him.

This simple yet moving account affords us the opportunity to note the difference between mercy and compassion. The blind men asked for God to act graciously toward them. Their plea for mercy is the plea for God not to forget God's promises, for God to do what God has promised. It is an appeal for God to be faithful to God's own history and commitment. Compassion contradicts nothing of this, but rather carries us into the heart of God, showing, as it were, God's vulnerability and suffering with all persons. Compassion in the New Testament carries with it the underlying reality of messianic solidarity with all who suffer. In other words, the blind men got more than they asked for. Jesus did not act only out of covenantal obligation and faithfulness, he felt with the men.

But it is in laying down the center of Christian service that this story has special value. Robert Gundry, in his commentary on Matthew's Gospel, remarks that compassion is added to this story by Matthew "in order to make the healing an act of service in line with vv. 20–28."[17] In compassion, Christian service must come out of a heart wounded by the suffering of others. This is in contrast to the self-serving assumptions of James and John.

The story tells us in a concrete way what servanthood is, what walking with Jesus means. It is surely no accident that the evangelist follows teaching on discipleship with a miracle performed on behalf of marginalized persons, persons who were allowed no rights by the crowd, not even the right to be ministered unto. A most eloquent expression of compassionate ministry to marginalized persons was written by Donald P. McNeill, Douglas A. Morrison, and Henri J. M. Nouwen in their beautiful book, *Compassion: A Reflection on the Christian Life.* "Compassion," they suggest,

> asks us to go where it hurts, to enter into places of pain, to share in brokenness, fear, confusion and anguish. Compassion challenges us to cry out with those in misery, to mourn with those who are lonely, to weep with those in tears. Compassion requires us to be weak with the weak, vulnerable with the vulnerable, and powerless with the powerless. Compassion means full immersion in the condition of being human.[18]

Later on in the book, the authors continue in a similar vein:

> Here we see what compassion means. It is not a bending toward the underprivileged from a privileged position; it is not a reaching out from on high to those who are less fortunate below; it is not a gesture of sympathy or pity for those who fail to make it in the upward pull. On the contrary, compassion means going directly to those people and places where suffering is most acute and building a home there.[19]

Compassion as we see it in this story (and in the story of the healing of the leper, discussed earlier) is a partisan solidarity with those who are on the margins of society. Jesus acted here with authority and showed clearly what his life and ministry were about. And in this miracle he challenged his disciples in their sense of calling and self-importance. Compassion is not an elective in the Christian faith; it is part of its very substance and integrity.

The Raising of the Son of the Widow of Nain
(Luke 7:11–17)

Luke 7:18 reads, "The disciples of John told him of all these things." And what follows is John's famous question of Jesus: "Are you he who is to come, or shall we look for another?", with the subsequent discussion on the person and work of Jesus. What John was told about and what constituted the context for this most important part of the Gospel is found in the two preceding narrative accounts: the healing of the centurion's servant (Luke 7:1–10) and the raising of the dead son of the widow of Nain (Luke 7:11–17). These two miracles occupy an important place in Luke's "narrative of the things which have been accomplished among us" (Luke 1:1). Luke is building up his answer to the Baptist's question concerning the identity of Jesus of Nazareth.

Jesus, his disciples, and a large crowd were approaching a town called Nain, in Galilee. Near the gate of the town they met a funeral procession en route to bury the dead son of a widow. The mention of the mother as a widow may be a reference to 1 Kings 17:10. Jesus, the Lord, saw the woman and had compassion on her. "Do not weep," he said (v. 13), perhaps in anticipation of the impending miracle. And then he touched the bier and commanded the dead man to arise. He sat up and, as if to emphasize his aliveness, Luke adds that he began to speak. With an echo of Elijah at 1 Kings 17:23, and perhaps to demonstrate his continuing compassion for the woman, Jesus gave the man back to his mother. Not surprisingly, the onlookers were awestruck and began to praise God.

Apart from the parable material, nowhere else in Luke-Acts does the evangelist use the verb "to have compassion." Even when Luke borrows from Mark, he does not use the word. What we seem to have here is an isolated unit of early tradition that Luke has incorporated into his Gospel. In that this passage is also the first recorded narrative reference by Luke to Jesus as "the Lord," it is clear that there was, from the very beginning of the church, the tradition that Jesus, the Lord, was the Compassionate One. Compassion, as we see it used here, is not simply the attribution of strong, sympathetic emotion to Jesus. It carries a theological significance in that it describes an aspect of his divinity. Compassion, in other words, is a messianic designation.[20]

"Are you he who is to come?" The compassion of Jesus is one way of answering that staggering question. Compassion, as the evangelists use it of Jesus, comes to mean Emmanuel, God with us.

A Summary of the Ministry of Jesus (Matthew 9:35–38)

These verses provide a conclusion to a section in Matthew's Gospel—8:1 through 9:34—in which the evangelist has gathered together narrative material that is scattered in Mark and Luke. The broad theme of the section is the authority of Jesus. Taking material from Mark 6:34, the first feeding story, Matthew expands it in line with his previous summary at 4:23.

We get a sense of the breadth of Jesus' ministry from this summary: teaching in synagogues, announcing the good news of the kingdom of God, and curing all kinds of diseases. Robert Gundry notes that "in order to satisfy two further interests of his—crowds as symbolic of those to be discipled from all nations and Jesus' compassion—Matthew now imports Mark 6:34 from the first part of the feeding of the five thousand."[21] We have already discussed what the image of sheep without a shepherd means. Matthew adds that they were also harassed and helpless. The total picture is one of people who were in a desperate state of spiritual exhaustion and confusion, who had no hope of relief.

We will conclude this discussion of compassion in the ministry of Jesus with a brief reflection on the quality of connectedness with another which it implies. Compassion, as we see it in these texts, is a ministry of presence.

To be present for another is to be available for him or her. It is to relate to another with all of one's attention and energy. And it is to invite that other into relationship with oneself. Presence allows another to stake a claim on one's personal and private space. It is to be open to being changed by another.

At various times all of us have been on the giving and receiving end of both presence and lack of presence. To experience presence is to feel that another is really taking you seriously. You matter to that person. His or her attention is really on you. You feel that you are significant for that person. This gives you the feeling of personal worth. To experience lack of presence is to feel that your personhood has little value. It is to feel self-esteem diminish and anger rise. You feel put down. A painful example of this can happen at a party, when one is in conversation with the host and realizes that he is in fact looking over one's shoulder to see if someone more important has come into the room.

Martin Buber, the Jewish philosopher and mystic, tells how once he received a visit from a student he had not met before. Buber confesses that in the interview he was not really present in spirit. While he did not fail to deal appropriately with the young man, he did not really attend to him. "I omitted to guess the questions which he did not put," Buber remarks. In other words, he was not present to him, listening between the lines. Later, Buber discovered that the young man committed suicide.[22]

Compassion as presence is not fulfilled simply by feeling the right feelings or by going through the motions of care. Compassion includes competence but is not reducible to it. The exercise of the technologies of care does not imply compassion. Buber recognized this after the fact. Compassion requires a quality of relationship, what we are calling "presence." It is the giving of oneself unconditionally. It is being wounded by the suffering of another.

Compassion as presence involves patience. As patience, presence is the gift of one's quality time. One gives away

one's time to another. One "wastes" time in compassionate presence. McNeill, Morrison, and Nouwen suggest that
patience is the discipline of compassion.[23] This is a willingness to hang tough with another. In other words, patience
is presence with fortitude. It is walking with another and
not giving up when the going becomes difficult or even
dangerous.

Simone Weil, the French philosopher and mystic, once
wrote that "those who are unhappy have no need for
anything in this world but people capable of giving them
their attention." Lest we think that presence is easy for
any of us, she goes on to remark that

> the capacity to give one's attention to a sufferer is a
> very rare and difficult thing; it is almost a miracle; it
> *is* a miracle. Nearly all those who think they have this
> capacity do not possess it. Warmth of heart, impulsive-
> ness, pity are not enough. . . .
>
> The love of our neighbour in all its fullness simply
> means being able to say to him: "What are you going
> through?" It is a recognition that the sufferer exists, not
> only as a unit in a collection, or a specimen from the
> social category labelled "unfortunate," but as a man,
> exactly like us, who was one day stamped with a special
> mark by affliction. For this reason it is enough, but it is
> indispensable, to know how to look at him in a certain
> way.
>
> This way of looking is first of all attentive. The soul
> empties itself of all its own contents in order to receive
> into itself the being it is looking at, just as he is, in all
> his truth.[24]

This is a profound statement on the nature, the possibility,
and the cost of compassion as presence.

It is of great significance that Matthew saw fit to use
compassion to describe the overarching response of Jesus
to the needs of the crowd. It was central to his mission. It
defined him in the depths of his being. It characterized the
quality of his relationships and what that quality cost him.
It described a way of being, a life-style if you like, in which

he was present for others in such a way that they were made whole. In the light of the texts we have discussed, we can conclude that there can be no adequate presentation of the ministry of Jesus of Nazareth which omits his compassion.

2

"Go and do likewise":
Compassion in the Teaching of Jesus

The verb "to have compassion" is used three times by
Jesus in parables to indicate the quality of God's concern
for the world. This quality of compassion must also mark
the life and service in those who would follow Jesus. Compassion does not only characterize the ministry of Jesus as
Lord; it must also characterize the lives of those who live
in him and who seek to be his disciples. Compassion is a
feature of our being "in Christ." It is not an ethical or
psychological disposition, something to have now and
then, as we allow our hearts to be warmed on occasion in
concern for another. Compassion is a part of what it means
to be a Christian.

In considering compassion in the teaching of Jesus, we
come face-to-face with something that represents Jesus'
claim upon our lives. We will explore later how compassion is possible at all for us. Here it is important to allow
the divine claim upon us to emerge in all its starkness,
unblurred by concerns over its practical possibility in our
lives.

There are three parables of compassion: Matthew 18:
23–35, the parable of the unforgiving debtor; Luke 10:30–
37, the parable of the good Samaritan; and Luke 15:11–32,
the parable of the prodigal son. Compassion plays a central
role in each parable, describing the action upon which the
parable turns.

Research and commentary on the parables are extensive and wide-ranging today. It is not the intention here to give a full account of the critical issues in interpretation as they emerge from that research, except insofar as they relate to our understanding of compassion. As before, we will discuss the biblical material with an eye to theological and pastoral concerns.

Jesus' parables are unique. According to J. Jeremias, nothing similar is to be found in rabbinic literature before Jesus. They take us close to the heart of Jesus' personal teaching style. "We stand right before Jesus when reading his parables."[1] In the Gospels, the parables are tools that Jesus used to engage in controversy, speaking to specific people in specific situations. They represent the cutting edge of Jesus' teaching ministry.

The Unforgiving Servant (Matthew 18:23–35)

This parable tells of a king who wished to put his fiscal affairs in order. During the accounting he discovered that one of his servants, possibly a high official, owed him a debt so large that it was quite beyond repayment. No larger amount of money could be imagined. In this there is an element of fantasy, which serves to highlight the munificence of the compassion the king will show. The king, first of all, however, ordered the servant and his family to be sold into slavery. At least he would get something back on the debt. Naturally distraught, and pleading for his very life, the servant fell on his knees and pleaded with the king, "Lord, have patience with me, and I will pay you everything" (v. 26). Of course, there is no likelihood whatsoever that he could repay the money owed. His promise, perhaps, was the product of fear and desperation. The king now was so moved with compassion (again, the RSV use of "pity" is inaccurate; *splanchnizomai* is properly translated "compassion") that he responded by canceling the debt and revoking the order to have the servant and his family sold off into slavery. Compassion, in this case, led to an astonishing act of mercy.

The focus of the drama turns now upon the servant. He

apparently was also owed a sum of money, but in contrast to the money he owed to the king, it was a paltry amount. Immediately upon his release from catastrophe he encountered his debtor. Violently he seized him by the throat and demanded repayment. Unlike the debt owed to the king, the debt owed to the servant was repayable. Repeating what had just happened earlier in the story, the servant's debtor fell on his knees and pleaded for patience so that the debt could be paid off in time. The servant, however, showed no compassion for his debtor. He remained unmerciful and hard-hearted and insisted upon his rights. He threw his debtor into jail for nonpayment of the debt until the amount owed was paid in full. By law his action was justified, although the contrast between the action of the king and the action of the servant obviously suggests the demand of a higher law.

As a kind of Greek chorus, the fellow servants, on hearing what had happened, reported to the king. The king, no doubt filled with righteous indignation, summoned his servant, reproached him for his behavior, and canceled the remission of his debt. The servant was handed over to the jailors to be tortured until he could repay what he owed. Because he would never be able to repay such a large amount, his punishment would be eternal.

The point of the story is obvious: We must show to others the mercy we have ourselves received from God. We cannot stand on our rights, for then God will stand on God's rights and the sentence that is rightly ours will be pronounced. Who then could be saved?

The crux of the action in the parable, that upon which all else depends, is the king's—that is, God's—compassion. Mercy (v. 33) is the consequence of compassion. Compassion, here at least, has a certain precedence over mercy.[2] It was compassion that made mercy possible, just as elsewhere it was compassion that made healing and teaching and feeding possible. However, God's compassion is not to be mocked. The God whose compassion is new every morning is also the judge, whose holy anger is righteous and severe. God's compassion upon us carries with it the divine demand that we be compassionate in turn. And there is an explicit "or else." The closing words of Jesus are stern: "So also my heavenly Father will do to every one of you, if you do not forgive your brother from your heart" (v. 35).

Our modern religious sensibilities may cause us to react with some repugnance to the sting at the end of the parable. Many of us have been brought up on a light theological diet, which leads us conveniently to consign "or else" injunctions to the edge of our understanding of God. We would like to think that the God of the New Testament is kind and gentle and friendly, no matter what. Yet the text invites us to reflect on the divine demand and the consequences if we fail to heed that demand. God's compassion will not be mocked.

Compassion in the parable is characteristic of the kingdom of God;[3] it teaches us about the nature of community that Christians must anticipate in the way they live their lives. The kingdom community has compassion at its center. If men and women relate to one another only out of legal obligation, while that might create a society, it does not create the kingdom community. In the community with compassion at its center we would relate to one another out of a fundamental solidarity and commitment that transcends private or individual rights. For the Christian, community means being the body of Christ, the household of faith, the *koinonia* of the Spirit. It means interconnection; it means relationship at the deepest level, perhaps even beyond our imagination. As Christians understand it, community is not the consequence of the equitable apportionment of private rights. Rather, community comes into being when persons relate compassionately, with the deepest sensitivity to the needs and suffering of others. It is in the compassionate community that we witness the in-breaking presence of the kingdom of God.

This corporate aspect of compassion is extraordinarily difficult to deal with, especially in a society founded upon individual rights, competition, and privacy. Further, the blunt facts of sin, fear, lack of trust, and the like make compassion and community virtually impossible for many of us. Of course, we all long for intimacy with others and for participation in compassionate communities. We want to belong, to feel accepted, even if in perversity we find ourselves doing those things that deny compassion and make community a longed-for but always elusive dream. Intimacy often remains, sadly, just a rare and fleeting experience, something we may have only occasionally with a very small circle of people. Day by day our experience is more likely to be of cutthroat competition, and we often feel brutalized by it. Popular wisdom teaches us that compassion has little place in business, commerce, politics, etc. And even if in the church we talk much about fellowship, the experience rarely matches our expectation, for few of us experience intimacy in our churches. In fact, there is little practical evidence to suggest that the church is in any way different from social groups in society with respect to the depth of and commitment to community.

Compassion, as we find it in this parable, is to be understood in terms of the coming of the kingdom of God. The vision of the compassionate community that it proclaims is the vision of the kingdom. We who live on this side of the fulfillment of the kingdom always live in tension, because we cannot reconcile the announcement of the kingdom and its demand, on the one hand, with the stark, blunt reality of life lived in the real world, on the other. There is a gap, as it were, between the promise and the fulfillment. This eschatological tension does not negate the validity of compassion for social ethics and community. Quite the opposite is in fact the case. But it does place the Christian in the enormously difficult and often painful situation of trying to live an ethic that seems at times to be impossible to fulfill. Life always imposes compromises upon us. And the way we want to live is not always the way we do live. We have ethical ambiguity over a host of issues. Yet the vision, promise, and demand of the kingdom are always before us, calling us into difficult obedience, calling us to live into the eschatological tension that will not be resolved until the kingdom is complete. Compassion is the impossible divine demand that calls us to live as kingdom people in a world that does not recognize, nurture, or admire such a way of life. The world, in fact, may well do everything to resist it. Living in the tension between the promise and the fulfillment, as we try to take compassion to all the world, we make witness to the compassion of God in Jesus Christ and the claim that makes upon us and all persons. When Christians try to live compassionate lives in the midst of the world, with all the ambiguity and complexity that this involves, this becomes a form of the divine criticizing of all those things in the world which are brutalizing. As Jürgen Moltmann once wrote with respect to hope, likewise we can say with respect to compassion: "Those who hope in Christ can no longer put up with reality as it is, but begin to suffer under it, to contradict it. Peace with God means conflict with the world, for the goad of the promised future stabs inexorably into the flesh of every unfulfilled present."[4] Compassion, wherever it is found, makes witness to God's dealings, God's demand, and God's kingdom promise, and thereby calls into question everything in the world, and also in the church, which is life-denying and community-destroying. Because it is of the substance of the kingdom of God, the Christian's struggling, often ambiguous compassion provokes a curious and disturbing incongruence in which the not-yet of the compassionate kingdom community stands in sharp contrast to the present form and experience of reality. Compassion, in other words, takes on the mantle of prophetic ministry.

The Good Samaritan (Luke 10:30–37)

More than just an ethical exhortation to reach out to those in need, this well-known parable addresses one of the most fundamental religious questions: What must I do to inherit eternal life? (Luke 10:25). Kenneth E. Bailey, who has devoted special study to the parables in Luke, argues convincingly that the parable should be read in the light of that question and the succeeding dialogue.[5] The parable is a part of the ongoing debate with the lawyer. Again, our concern is not to understand all aspects of the parable, but to attend to what it has to teach us about compassion.

A man, probably a Jew, was traveling from Jerusalem to Jericho, a road notorious for its danger. He was attacked violently, robbed, stripped naked, and left for dead. There was little now to give him religious, ethnic, or social identity.[6] He represents every person in need. A priest, most certainly riding and therefore, in principle, able to render aid, passed by the injured traveler but did not render the assistance that common decency would have demanded. All kinds of religious and cultural reasons have been advanced for this pastoral failure. In all likelihood the priest was the victim of a rule-book orthodoxy; he cared by the rules. His principles of behavior were prescribed and inviolable. A similar lack of attention was shown by the second passerby, a Levite, a man lower in the temple hierarchy and more free therefore to render aid without violating the regulations. He too saw the injured traveler by the roadside. And he too did not render aid.

Jesus' hearers now anticipated a third traveler, probably a Jewish layman. Is the parable to be an attack on clericalism? Jesus' audience probably hoped so. Bailey goes to some length to show how utterly shocking the introduction of a hated Samaritan would have been. Jesus spoke to his audience's deepest racial and religious prejudice and dramatically exposed it.[7] And Jesus made the Samaritan the hero of the story, showing that compassion, this divine characteristic that has its source in the womb of Yahweh, was appropriate even for those beyond the fold. The ghetto of closed-minded religious intolerance is broken open to show that compassion is a universal demand. Jesus, comments Jeremias, "had intentionally chosen an extreme example; by comparing the failure of the ministers of God with the unselfishness of the hated Samaritan, his hearers should be able to measure the absolute and unlimited nature of the duty of love."[8]

The Samaritan had compassion on the wounded traveler. He too risked the ritual contamination that the priest and the Levite probably feared so much. By pausing on his journey to render aid, he too risked attack from the robbers who may still have lurked nearby. Bailey suggests that he probably knew of the priest's and Levite's failure to act.[9] Regardless, his gut-level response to the traveler moved him into concrete, saving action.

"The center of the parable," says Bailey, "displays the unexpected appearance of the compassionate Samaritan. The rest of the action is the expression of that compassion."[10] The binding of wounds and the pouring of oil were profound, theologically significant acts of ministry, alluding both to God's saving work and to the worship of the temple. The Samaritan, in fact, was the true priest. The placing of the injured man on the riding animal was the act of a servant. Taking the traveler thereafter to an inn was an act of mercy and courage. The assumption would have been that perhaps Samaritan robbers had perpetrated the original crime and by law and custom the family of the injured traveler could have sought redress from the one rendering aid. Anyone who became involved in helping the victim of an accident could be considered partially, if not totally, responsible. Why did he stop?—seems to be a fair question. Bailey suggests an evocative cultural parallel: Imagine a Plains Indian in 1875 walking into Dodge City with a scalped cowboy draped over his horse![11]

Caution would have been prudent, and the Samaritan would have been adjudged wise had he left the injured traveler outside the inn and made a hasty and furtive retreat. But casting caution and prudence aside, and in obedience to a higher law—the demand of compassion—the Samaritan persevered with his act of mercy, committing himself even to a return journey to ensure the traveler's well-being. "The Samaritan is an unknown stranger. Yet, in spite of the cost in time, effort, money, and personal danger, he freely demonstrates unexpected love to the one in need. Is not this a dramatic demonstration of the kind of love God offers through His unique agent in the Gospel?"[12]

Bailey sums up the point of the parable of the good Samaritan in this way: "I must *become* a neighbor to anyone in need. To fulfill the law means that I must reach out in costly compassion to all people, even to my enemies. The standard remains even though I can never fully achieve it. I cannot justify myself and earn eternal life."[13]

Compassionate service may well lead us beyond what may be regarded as an acceptable or prudent level of involvement with another in need to a level of involvement that could demand great personal cost. Time and again Jesus broke the canons of respectable self-limiting behavior. We have seen this already in the account of Jesus' healing of the leper at Mark 1:40–45. No self-respecting Jew would have acted as he frequently acted, keeping company with the money men, the prostitutes, the poor, the deranged, and the other marginalized persons in his community. His compassion often led him beyond the acceptable limits of pastoral orthodoxy. In his teaching of the parable of the good Samaritan, Jesus shows that compassion, in fact, may well lead to a risk-filled pastoral unorthodoxy. Truth, in other words, can appropriately be found in right doing (orthopraxy) as well as in right believing (orthodoxy).

The parable demonstrates what compassion demands of us. And it leaves us in no doubt over the possible personal cost. Once and for all we can see that compassion is not a feeling of sympathy or, even less so, of pity. There is nothing wimpish, bland, or weak-minded about compassion. And there is no indication whatsoever of superiority, of the stronger person helping the weaker in a condescending or demeaning way. The compassion of the Samaritan demonstrates a profound depth of solidarity and a constancy of commitment that mark compassion as a tough-minded, courageous, and rigorous work of ministry in which the limits of prudence are rolled back. The compassionate person does not go by the book!

Compassion may well lead one into gray areas of unconventionality and risk. In compassion one names the "pastoral forgetting" that can become so convenient. It is not difficult to be blinkered or blinded with respect to street people, chemical abusers, the mentally ill, those who have failed in the upward march, the poor, the aged, and the children—indeed, all of those whom Jesus called "the least of the brethren." There is no guarantee that compassionate service will ever be fashionable or that it will help one in one's career; it seems reasonable to suggest, in fact, that compassion may cause one also to be cast out, to become marginalized oneself. And if compassion is pursued with an uncompromising sense of commitment to see it through to the end, it is quite likely that one will be led into conflict with the keepers of the parameters of pastoral propriety—the priest and the Levite, those who represent a religious hierarchy. Compassion will, by example and implication, name the inadequacy of these parameters and thereby call into question the structures of ecclesiastical power and theological control that make pastoral forgetting possible. The compassionate person does not care by the rules. He or she marches to a different drummer. And in this, compassion becomes a confrontative and a prophetic ministry. Jeremias remarks that "the scribe is thinking of himself, when he asks: What is the limit of my responsibility? (v. 29). Jesus says to him: Think of the sufferer, put yourself in his place, consider, Who needs help from me? (v. 36). Then you will see that love's demand knows no limit."[14]

The parable of the good Samaritan points us to the heart of God. As Bailey indicates, the early exegetes identified the good Samaritan with Jesus. "The overtones of Christology are in the parable itself. . . . Is it not possible here to touch something of Jesus' own understanding of his ministry as God's unique agent who comes as a suffering servant to save?"[15] Only God in Christ can pick up every wounded traveler and not be destroyed by the extent of shared suffering. Only Jesus is required to take the risk of carrying the pain of the whole world upon his shoulders.

In this, he is alone, truly, the Compassionate One. Jesus is compassion incarnate; he is God with us in this astonishing depth of caring for and solidarity with each of us within the self-limitation of his chosen humanity. In part, compassion identifies and defines his messiahhood. We, in our turn, can only be compassionate in him by sharing in his compassion. Nowhere does the New Testament say that anyone other than Jesus acted with compassion. Yet he demands the impossible possibility of us. The parable makes that quite clear. Full discussions of the compassion of God and the compassion of the Christian as his or her participation in the compassion of Christ will be found in later chapters.

The Prodigal Son (Luke 15:11-32)

This powerful parable has been called *Evangelium in Evangelio*, a summary of the Gospel, containing all of the major themes: sin, repentance, grace, compassion, joy, restoration, "sonship" and the searching, saving love of God.[16] And probably more than anywhere else in the New Testament, this parable indicates the profound inner connection between compassion and the suffering of God. The parable, in other words, takes us close to the divine heart of compassion, laying bare before us the cost to God of reaching into the far country of our lostness. Under pressure from the parable, as its truth presses in on our minds, we will find that we have to stretch our understanding of compassion to the limit, reaching out in the last analysis to redefine it. In this way, our developing exploration of the meaning of compassion is bounded and controlled by the biblical word itself.

The younger son in a family asks for and receives his inheritance and the right to dispose of it in any way he sees fit. This request and its granting are highly unusual. The request means that the younger son wants his father to die. Surely the father should be angry at such an awful request. However, instead of punishment the loving father grants the request in an astonishing act of parental love. The elder son is noticeable in his silence, refusing to act as an agent of reconciliation. Both sons have failed their father.

The young man sells his inheritance, leaves home, and soon loses it all. His sin, as he sees it, is the loss of the money and his failure to be a dutiful son in being able to care for his family. Poverty reduces him to tending pigs, a terrible indignity. He is forced even to eat their food to keep himself alive. He decides to return to his village and perhaps to work his way back into his family's good graces. He is, of course, apprehensive about his return.

However, his reception is not as he expected it would be. He is overwhelmed by his father's public display of love. He is offered irresistible grace; he confesses his sin; he accepts restoration to sonship. The community rejoices.

The older son, however, is unable to cope with his father's love for and forgiveness of his younger brother. His father extends the same love toward him, but he does not confess his sin and return to fellowship. Instead, he upbraids his father in his bitterness. The parable ends with an appeal by the father for reconciliation. The Pharisee listening to the story is led to conclude, surely, that he is the elder son.[17]

The center of the story is the compassion which the father has for his returning younger son as he sees him far off (v. 20). It is important to look at the father in some detail in order to grasp clearly the depth of his compassion.

First of all, the father showed astonishing love in granting the wish of his younger son. The request amounted to a break in their relationship. The youngster cut himself off from his family and community. By his own act he chose to become "lost," to live in the far country. In spite of his son's rejection of his fatherhood, the father chose to continue to be father to his son. The relationship was broken from the son's side only. Bailey notes that "if the father had disowned the son then there would be no possibility of reconciliation. The father's suffering provides the foundation of the possibility of the son's return."[18] The father took the son's rejection into himself, as it were, and this must have deepened profoundly his own suffering. The son's return and restoration is predicated precisely on the father's willingness to continue to suffer for his son.

Second, the father acted in an amazing manner at the son's homecoming. The purpose of the drama of the story at this point, centering on the father's compassion for the son, is the restoration of the youth to fellowship within the community.[19] Publicly, the father refused to stand on his rights. Instead, he showed the depth of his love for his son by offering to restore the relationship *from his side*. He who had done no wrong became the one who bore the cost of reconciliation. By his actions he made reconciliation possible. Only the father could heal what the son had broken. As Bailey notes, "the text says. 'He had compassion.' We would suggest that this 'compassion' specifically includes awareness of the gauntlet the boy will have to face as he makes his way through the village. The father then runs the gauntlet for him."[20] It is an overwhelming act of grace, mirroring the vicarious humanity of God in Christ. From the father's side, it was costly reconciliation, for the father not only went out to meet his son but publicly humiliated himself in the process. And by his action he showed the whole community that he had forgiven his son. "The father in the story forgives through suffering, for there is no forgiveness without suffering. Sin cannot be borne away until it is borne. The father illustrates this principle in his response to his son from the beginning to the end of the story."[21]

It is hardly accidental that this is a significant theme also in the parable of the unforgiving debtor at Matthew 18: 23–35. There, the compassionate king refused to stand on his rights and had to suffer the loss of the money that was rightfully his. He had to cover the debt. He bore the cost. The connection between compassion and atonement that we find in these two parables takes the work of salvation deeply into God's own being—not just into God's will, so to speak, into God's heart, or, better, into God's womb, as we will see in the next chapter. Compassion allows us to see something of the cost and pain of atonement for God.

Christological themes can be overheard in the action of the father. Jeremias notes that, in the parable, Jesus *"claims that in his actions the love of God to the repentant sinner is made effectual.* Thus the parable, without making any kind of christological statement, reveals itself as a veiled assertion of authority: Jesus makes the claim for himself that he is acting in God's stead, that he is God's representative."[22] And the soteriology of sin-bearing for another in suffering love, of course, is a prefiguration of the cross. "When the father leaves the house to come out to his son in love and humility, he demonstrates at least a part of the meaning of the incarnation and the atonement."[23]

Third, as we saw earlier, in the account of the healing of the epileptic youth at Mark 9:14–29, compassion has an evangelical dimension in which an appropriate response is called forth from the one healed. Compassion is not cheap grace. Similarly in this parable, the father's compassion calls forth and makes possible the son's repentance. In view of the father's preemptive love, the son knew he had nothing to offer. He could only accept what was offered. The son responded to the father's prevenient grace. Repentance followed grace; indeed, it was possible only on the ground created by grace. It is the indicative (I love you and have compassion on you) that conditions the imperative (Repent and amend your life). To repeat: There is nothing the son could have done from his side. Reconciliation had to happen from the father's side, from the side of the innocent party. That is why it is grace. It was pure gift. Yet following grace, the demand was total. Grace demanded repentance, demanded response.

Fourth, in the second half of the parable, the account of the father and the older son, we find the same theological dynamics that occurred in the first half: a lost son, a humiliated father who tried to love the son into reconciliation, and the response, which now is negative. While the entreating love of the father is not described as compassionate, it most surely was. The father's response to his older son came out of a wounded, suffering heart. "The Christological implications of this second section are the same as those of the first section," writes Bailey. "The father leaves the house in visible demonstration of unexpected love offered in humiliation. The same implicit Christology 'overheard' in the first half of the parable can be found here as well."[24]

What does the parable of the prodigal son (a better naming would be the parable of the compassionate father) teach us about compassion? As noted above, we see a profound connection between compassion and suffering. But it is suffering of a particular kind and with a specific end in view. In fact, the link between compassion and suffering in the parable serves as a metaphor for incarnation and atonement, taking us into the inner heart of God in salvation. We find here that we must include a soteriological dimension in our understanding of the meaning of compassion.

Compassion is conventionally defined as suffering with another person. We have had no reason to alter that definition so far; our concern has been to explore its depth and appreciate its radicality. In its soteriological dimension, however, compassion means not only "suffering with another" but also "suffering for another." In compassion, one may carry the sin and suffering of others in such a way that they may be restored to wholeness precisely because their sin and suffering are borne. As such, compassion is a priestly ministry of vicarious suffering. One's compassionate solidarity with the suffering of another becomes a redemptive solidarity. It is an entry into the depths of another's lostness, displacement, and separation. And because of the journey of the compassionate one into the far country of another's lostness, through compassion and suffering, a redemptive bond is established which can bring that other home.

Compassion as "suffering for" is supremely Christ's ministry. As the Compassionate One, he alone makes atonement for the sin of the world. However, as Christians find their life ever more deeply in him, one would expect that

even this vicarious dimension of compassion would begin
to come to expression in the ministry of the church. Here
compassion moves far beyond simply caring for people. It
becomes in and through Jesus Christ a priestly ministry of
redemption.

Epilogue to Chapters 1 and 2: Compassion Is Not Mercy, Empathy, Sympathy, or Pity

As we have noted, compassion is commonly lumped
together with perceived synonyms like mercy, empathy,
sympathy, and pity. Many theological dictionaries and
commentaries also make this mistake, adding to the conceptual confusion and to the blunting of the particularity
of compassion. This carelessness contributes to the already
considerable neglect of compassion, causing it to remain
hidden behind other concepts.

Mercy is a powerful biblical word. It is used frequently
and has great weight. While it is similar to compassion in
a general way, it really has its own separate meaning and
significance.

The biblical concept of mercy is related to the Hebrew
understanding of the covenant made by God with Israel.
At its root, mercy has a legal basis. It means covenantal
loyalty or faithfulness. And because God is understood
quite properly as the superior in the covenant relationship, God's faithfulness keeps the covenant in being.
Mercy is an act of grace in which God remains faithful
even when the people turn aside from God and are un-
faithful to the covenant.

It is this idea of God's in-breaking loyalty in the face of
disloyalty that lies behind the New Testament notion of
mercy. Jesus Christ is God's mercy incarnate. He is God's
final and complete act of faithfulness, making a new covenant with us, sealed in his blood.

Mercy refers to God's faithfulness. It is an act of the
divine will. Compassion, on the other hand, refers to God's
experience of suffering with the people's suffering. Clearly
mercy and compassion overlap (see Matt. 18:27, 33) and

we ought not to be too doctrinaire in keeping them apart. Yet they are like two tributaries feeding into the one river; each has its own source, even if the water is the same. If we keep the distinctions between mercy and compassion in mind, allowing each its own particularities as we notice also points of similarity, each is the stronger for the conceptual clarity.

Empathy also is a special word, a word denoting great depth of relationship and healing. It refers to the entry into another person's frame of reference, into his or her world, in such a way that one can understand from the inside, so to speak, what that other is feeling. Empathy is a basic resource for both pastoral counseling and psychotherapy. It is by empathy that the counselor enters into the affective world of the client. The counselor is tuned in to the client's feelings. It is the communication of the counselor to the client that he or she "hears" the other's feelings which often enables healing to begin. The fact that a client feels that the counselor "hears" and accepts his or her feelings, and especially the negative feelings, is one of the significant points of breakthrough in counseling.

Empathy has been nurtured in our day as a primary resource for psychologically sensitive healing love. And in many ways it is similar to compassion. Empathy in counseling can of course be a significant way in which a person's compassion can be translated into ministry. Both involve a deep involvement in the feelings of another person.

But there are significant points of difference between empathy and compassion. To begin with, empathy is not a biblical word and not, therefore, a word that has a theological history. Compassion, on the other hand, is a profound biblical word with a clear theological identity, as we have seen. Second, compassion is a ministry which for the Christian is entirely and uniquely rooted in Jesus Christ. Empathy has a legitimacy and worth quite apart from any religious identification whatsoever. Third, Christians and Jews are all called to be compassionate, as God is compassionate. Obedience in faith requires it. Empathy, at least as it is used today, has become a highly specialized and professional tool for ministry. It is a technical resource. One would not speak of the empathy of all believers; one could refer, however, to the empathy of all psychotherapists. This is not a criticism of empathy. It merely indicates the difference between empathy and compassion.

Compassion is not sympathy. Sympathy is a biblical word, and it shares some aspect with compassion. It means having pathos for another, and that is very similar to compassion. However, the word is not used directly of Jesus in the New Testament. That is not to say that sympathy is not an important human emotion. But there is little biblical basis for constructing a theology of sympathy. Further, sympathy seems to keep things at the level of shared feelings, and it implies little sense of active involvement in ministry which we found always to be the case with compassion. This does not mean that sympathy is a second-class word. It has its own value. So, although sympathy and compassion have points of similarity, each is distinct and the two should not be confused.

Finally, it is important to distinguish compassion from pity. Of all the words similar to compassion in common use, pity is the most dangerous. Yet it is disturbing to see how often compassion and pity are used interchangeably, as if they shared the same meaning. To take just one unfortunate example: *The New English Bible* translates Matthew 9:36, a text that sums up the Lord's ministry, by using the word "pity." The Greek word used in the text, in fact, is *splanchnizomai*—compassion, not pity.

The change in meaning is very significant. Pity is a hierarchical concept. It implies a looking down upon another. It is condescension. Pity arises out of the maintenance of distance between people. It has nothing of the adventure of intimacy and commitment that are essential to compassion. Separateness, and not relationship, is the essence of pity. Further, pity makes another dependent and passive, reducing that person to the level of a child acted upon by a superior-feeling adult. Friedrich Nietzsche once remarked that "pity is the practice of nihilism." Compassion, we would suggest, is the very opposite; it is the practice of life. Pity, then is an unacceptable concept; it is a kind of theological four-letter word, a word that should not be a part of our theological vocabulary.[25]

Compassion has its own meaning, its unique identity. It has points of similarity with mercy, empathy, and sympathy, but it has a distinct meaning apart from these concepts. We will play our part in rescuing compassion from neglect if we keep these conceptual distinctions in mind.

3

The Wounded, Ministering God:
A Theology of Divine Compassion

Jesus was compassionate. Compassion marked both his pastoral ministry and his teaching. And he called those who would follow him to be compassionate as he was compassionate. The question for us to consider now is: How is God involved in Jesus' compassion, and how does that affect our basic understanding of God? Clearly the issue of the compassion of God is critical. The integrity and authority of compassion as a theological concept, as well as the integrity and authority of a considerable part of Jesus' ministry, stands or falls on the issue of God's capacity for compassion.

Since the very beginning of Christian theology, the church has taught the doctrine of God's freedom from change and suffering. J. K. Mozley, for example, argued for "the existence of a steady and continuous, if not quite unbroken, tradition in Christian theology as to the freedom of the divine nature from all suffering and from any potentiality of suffering."[1] Developing a doctrine of God's compassion inevitably involves a departure from the steady stream of theological tradition. Obviously, if we cannot speak properly of the suffering of God, we cannot speak at all, except perhaps metaphorically and allusively, of the compassion of God.

Christian talk of God grew out of the immensely fruitful interaction between the intellectual concepts and categories of the Greek philosophical traditions and the Hebrew faith and tradition that culminated in Jesus Christ. From the beginning, Christianity sought to think through and present its claims in critical dialogue with the prevailing Greek philosophical culture. This we find already in the New Testament, which was written in Greek and which often used Greek concepts and images to express the truth of the gospel. There were also apologetical and evangelical issues at stake, for the gospel had to be defended and proclaimed in critical dialogue with the existing religious and intellectual culture. Inevitably, therefore, Christianity and Greek culture and ideas reacted with one another in the crucible of debate.

A highly significant doctrine of God emerged out of this dialogue, a doctrine that has largely endured through the centuries and still carries considerable force even today. The rather auspicious name given to this historical doctrine of God is "classical theism." An insight derived from Greek philosophy was its original source.

The Greeks taught a doctrine of perfection that applied to God or, indeed, to any truth. That which is true is perfect. It is entirely complete; it is adequate. That which is perfect is beyond change; it cannot change to become more perfect; any change would only serve to diminish its perfection. Perfection implies unchangeability—or, to give it its philosophical designation, immutability.

The early church encountered this philosophical idea of the unchangeability of God as an irresistible axiom.[2] God's unchangeable perfection was expressed by the word *apatheia*, apathy, which means that God was thought to be incapable of being acted upon. *Apatheia* is a state of eternal stability. This meant that God could not be swayed in one direction or another. God could not be diverted or unsettled by the vagaries of passion or thought. God, in other words, could not be affected by anything in the world.

The importance of this point is that apathy, as we will see in the next chapter, is the opposite of compassion. The apathy of God inspires an ethical ideal of unaffected love. Jürgen Moltmann notes that "if it is the moral ideal of the wise man to become similar to the divinity and participate in its sphere, he must overcome needs and drives and lead a life free of trouble and fear, anger and love, in *apatheia.*"³

It is now just a short step from the doctrine of the immutability of God—God does not change—to the doctrine of the impassibility of God—God does not suffer. In fact, the former implies and demands the latter. The apathetic God or person is free from being affected by the pathos of life. This is a God or person unacquainted with suffering and for whom, therefore, compassion is an impossibility.

As an illustration of what this means, consider Anselm, the medieval theologian who, on this issue at least, gets himself tied into a terrible tangle. Anselm shows what God's inability to suffer means with respect to God's capacity for compassion.

> How art Thou at once pitiful and impassible? For if Thou art impassible, Thou dost not suffer with man; if Thou dost not suffer with man, Thy heart is not wretched by compassion with the wretched, which is the meaning of being pitiful. But if Thou art not pitiful, whence can the wretched gain so great a comfort? How then art Thou, and art Thou not pitiful, Lord, except that Thou art pitiful in respect of us, and not in respect of Thyself? Truly Thou art so in respect of our feeling, but are not in respect of Thine. For when Thou lookest upon us in our wretchedness we feel the effect of Thy pity, Thou feelest not the effect. And therefore Thou art pitiful, because Thou savest the wretched, and sparest the sinners who belong to Thee; and Thou art not pitiful, because Thou art touched by no fellow-suffering in that wretchedness.⁴

The God of classical theism has been beautifully praised in Walter Chalmers Smith's well-known hymn, "Immortal, Invisible, God Only Wise." Classical images abound: "in light inaccessible"; "unresting, unhasting, and silent as light, nor wanting nor wasting"; "nought changeth Thee." The Westminster Confession of Faith, 2.1, describes God as "a most pure spirit, invisible, without body, parts, or passions, immutable, immense, eternal, incomprehensible, almighty." Clearly, classical theism is a lively part of our theological heritage.

We must not be too quick to criticize this classical doctrine of God. It intended to present a God who was eternal, who was above and beyond all that was passing and temporary. The idea was not to focus on an inert, distant deity but rather to express the view that God was not so wholly bound up with the caprices of history as to become incapacitated and overwhelmed. However, not only did it lead to a view of God's inability to suffer, and therefore to God's inability to have compassion, it led also to serious problems in the understanding of the identity of Jesus Christ. If Jesus was wholly God, as Christian theology maintains, then as God he did not fully enter into the human condition. He suffered in his humanity only, but not in his divinity. This is to present a dualistic understanding of Christ in which his personhood is ripped in two.

If compassion is to be rooted in the being of God, obviously an alternative to the classical doctrine of God's freedom from suffering will have to be found. We require a revolution in our understanding of the nature of God.

The Suffering of God in the Old Testament

The millennia-old doctrine that God neither changes nor suffers is coming under considerable attack today. Although modern theology inherited the traditional doctrine, it has all but been replaced by an emerging theological consensus that sees the divinity of God, at least to some degree, in God's capacity for suffering. In this the theologians today have recovered an understanding of God that was woven into the texture of the Old Testament. The God of the Bible is not the distant, autonomous, untouched deity of Greek philosophy but the passionate, affected, and fiercely loving covenantal God who is revealed first in the history of God's dialogue with Israel.

While it would be incorrect to collapse our understanding of God in the Old Testament into any one category, it is now increasingly "clear that suffering belongs to the person and purpose of God."[5] One of the first students of the Bible in modern times who explicitly contested the doctrine of God's freedom from suffering was Abraham Heschel in his study of the prophets.[6] The prophet, writes Heschel, "dwells upon God's inner motives. . . . He discloses *a divine pathos,* not just a divine judgment. The pages of the prophetic writings are filled with echoes of divine love and disappointment, mercy and indignation. . . . This divine pathos is the key to inspired prophecy."[7] God, argues Heschel, operates out of pathos. "Pathos, concern for the world, is the very ethos of God."[8]

It is interesting that Heschel focused the suffering of God in God's capacity for pathos. (Augustine, representing classical theism, called pathos "a movement of the mind contrary to reason" and thereby incompatible with blessedness.[9]) Pathos, the capacity for and openness to suffering, and the opposite of a-pathos, or apathy, is obviously a prerequisite for com-pathos, compassion. It is with Heschel, then, that we begin to see that compassion may be appropriately predicated of God. Commenting on Heschel's "pathetic theology," Moltmann remarks that "God is affected by events and human actions and sufferings in history. . . . The history of the divine *pathos* is embedded in the history of men."[10]

A recent study by Terence E. Fretheim, *The Suffering of God: An Old Testament Perspective,* which is indebted to Heschel's work, helpfully gathers and interprets the biblical material. While a thorough review of Fretheim's study is beyond the scope of this discussion, it meets our purpose to summarize the parts of the book that deal explicitly with our theme.

Fretheim orders his material according to a threefold schema:

1. God suffers *because* of the people's rejection of God as Lord.
2. God suffers *with* the people who are suffering.
3. God suffers *for* the people.[11]

While these categories have a source in early material, it is in the prophets, as we saw briefly in Heschel's work, that we find the preponderance of references to divine suffering. "While a distinction between prophet and God must be maintained, the prophet's suffering mirrors the suffering of God before the people. God is present not only in the word which the prophet speaks, but also in the word as embodied in the prophet's life. In a sense, those who hear *and see* the prophet, hear and see God."[12] The sufferings of the prophet and God are so interwoven that they cannot be meaningfully separated.

First, then, God suffers *because* of the people's rejection. God grieves because the people have turned away. "As for the content of the grieving, the associated ideas in passages which speak of human grieving are striking: forsakenness (Isa. 54:6); mourning (2 Sam. 19:3); distress and anger (Gen. 45:5); injury (Ps. 56:5). The verb points to a considerable range in the divine response to the rejection by the people."[13] Isaiah 63:7–10 recalls a God who grieves because the people have rebelled, a God who acts in both anger and compassion. "It is God in all his Godness who grieves," observes Fretheim.[14] Genesis 6:5–6 recalls a divine grieving that goes back to the morning of the world. God, then, is open to and affected by the world. God is not apathetic. In a quite beautiful image, Fretheim comments that "grief is always what the Godward side of judgment looks like."[15]

As God remembers the faithfulness of Israel, in contrast to the present, there is further occasion for divine suffering. Jeremiah 2:2 is a picture of the pain and anguish of God:

> I remember the devotion of your youth,
>   your love as a bride,
> how you followed me in the wilderness,
>   in a land not sown.

Similarly, Jeremiah 2:29–32 shows how God, in living with the question "Why?", endures continuing anguish. Jeremiah 3:19–20 is almost overwhelming in its pathos. God has experienced rejection as both parent and as husband! "God," notes Fretheim, "suffers the effects of the broken relationship at multiple levels of intimacy. The wounds of God are manifold."[16]

The memory of God comes to poignant expression in Hosea 11. Here God's love is such that it will not let go. Even amid rejection and sorrow and anger, God's love endures, steadfast in its purpose summed up at verse 1: "When Israel was a child, I loved him."

Finally, God asks the question of all who suffer: How long? (Num. 14:27; Jer. 4:14; 13:27; Hos. 8:5). "It is clear from the laments of the psalter (e.g., Ps. 6:3; 13:1–2) that this question cannot be interpreted as a straightforward request for information; it represents a cry that contains two key elements: complaint with respect to something that is believed to have gone on long enough, and anguish over the abandonment and its seeming finality."[17] The lament draws on past intimacy now no longer experienced. Memory intensifies the pain; it is bittersweet.

In summary, these texts give us a glimpse into the heart of God. God is wounded by broken relationships. What has happened in the world has made a difference to God. But God is not overwhelmed or embittered. God's saving purpose does not waver. God continues to love the people and to seek their good.

Second, God suffers *with* the people. This is first seen in the exodus. At Exodus 3:7 we read that God knows the suffering of the people in slavery in Egypt. It is an intimate knowing, in the sense of knowing from the inside, as it were. But God is not powerless in the face of this knowledge. God moves to deliver, to redeem. God's suffering with the people is usually expressed in the language of mourning and compassion. Amos 5:1–2 shows that it is God's sorrow through the prophet which is intended to move the people to repentance, not threat. At Isaiah 15 and 16 God mourns for Moab. Selected verses speak for themselves:

> My heart cries out for Moab. . . .
> Therefore I weep with the weeping of Jazer. . . .
> I drench you with my tears. . . .
> Therefore my soul moans like a lyre for Moab,
> and my heart for Kir-heres.

Fretheim comments: "To hear such mourning on the part of God for a non-Israelite people is striking indeed."[18]

At Jeremiah 31:20, God takes on the role of mother in place of Rachel. As Rachel remembers and weeps for her children, so also God remembers and weeps, although God is not incapacitated, for God will turn the mourning into joy.[19]

In summary, God, in the face of Israel's judgment, takes up the cry of a mourner. Also, God immediately turns from the role of judge to that of fellow sufferer. For judgment means death for Israel. It is only God's redemptive action that can restore Israel to wholeness.[20]

Third, God suffers *for* the people. Here Fretheim steps lightly, for there is no doctrine of the atonement as such in the Old Testament. Yet there are prefigurations. By carrying the sins of the people on God's own shoulders, God suffers, in a sense, on their behalf, halting the judgment that was justly deserved. Fretheim also notes the divine weariness, the expending of the divine life, in the face of the people's faithlessness. But there is a divine restraint (Isa. 48:9; Ezek. 20:21–22; Ps. 78:38; and Isa. 57:11). God has internalized the people's rejection and this occasions profound weariness. God's suffering here does not yet mean redemption, but it does mean life.[21] God does not deal with the people according to the demands of the Law, but graciously, choosing to extend the divine suffering rather than bringing Israel to judgment.

It is clear from Fretheim's discussion, of which only a brief part has been presented, that any view of God that is grounded in the Old Testament must include some notion of the suffering of God. It would be a violation of biblical language to suggest otherwise. We see through the biblical language to the reality of a suffering God. The Old Testament bids us to understand God in terms of God's involvement with the world and reveals that God is profoundly affected by suffering with and for the people of Israel, God's own people.

The Wounded Womb of God

Rabbi Samuel H. Dresner cites a beautiful Jewish prayer, a prayer of God himself: "May it be My will that My compassion might overcome Mine anger and prevail over My justice, that I might deal with My children according to the attitude of compassion."[22] Building on the general background of God's capacity for suffering in the Old Testament, we turn now to look briefly at the Hebrew understanding of God's compassion.

The great declaration of Exodus 34:6 tells us that the Lord is a God of tenderness and compassion. This verse is echoed in Psalm 78:38 and is the theme of Psalm 103. Lamentations 3:22–23 proclaims that God's never-failing compassion is new every morning. Both Deuteronomy 13:17 and 30:3 refer to God's compassion in response to the people's disobedience. Because of God's covenant with Abraham, Isaac, and Jacob, God turned with compassion toward Israel and would not cast them from the divine presence or destroy them (2 Kings 13:23).

Isaiah 49:15 gives us a profound insight into the Hebrew meaning of compassion. The verse reads: "Can a woman forget her sucking child, that she should have no compassion on the son of her womb? Even these may forget, yet I will not forget you." A similar connection between maternity and compassion is found at Exodus 2:6: "When she [Pharaoh's daughter] opened it [the basket] she saw the child; and lo, the babe was crying. She took pity [i.e., compassion] on him." The connection between maternity and compassion is not incidental to our understanding of compassion in the Old Testament.

The Hebrew word for compassion is *rachamim*. It certainly describes a powerful emotion of deep concern for the welfare of another. Unlike our common connection of emotion with the heart, however, the Hebrews connected emotions with the lower viscera, the organs located in the abdominal cavity. The innards or bowels were the seat of the sympathetic emotions in general. In their customary physical, fleshly way, the Hebrews, when they felt emotion, felt it deeply within their bodies.

There is yet another element to *rachamim*, however, which particularizes the seat of compassion in a quite remarkable way. *Rachamim* is derived from another Hebrew word, *rechem*, which means womb or uterus. The literal meaning of compassion, then, is the womb pained in solidarity with the suffering of another. The feeling of deep kinship with another is understood now in an intimate and physical way as the wounding of the womb. The wounded womb is the core of the biblical meaning of compassion.

At its most basic, compassion represents a feminine characteristic of God, if it is appropriate to speak of God in such anthropomorphic language. Compassion describes God's mothering solidarity with God's people. The notion of God's compassion as the wounding of the womb of God is a somewhat unnerving notion, and one a man may only approach with some sensitivity to the fact that the reference is quite beyond his biological experience. Indeed, to speak of the interior experience of God here as the wounding of God's womb is quite beyond any human imagining. Yet the biblical image of compassion compels us to suggest that it refers to God's deepest and most creative—we might even say life-giving—suffering with the people. There is great beauty in the image, and great pathos. And it is this pathos, this element of intense, vulnerable suffering, that we must ever keep before us, lest in forgetting it we thereby sentimentalize compassion and rob it of its power and energy.

On the basis of the Old Testament, we can conclude that God is intimately acquainted with suffering and that in compassion God is affected in God's deepest inner being. It is not surprising, then, to find that compassion has been woven into the fabric of Judaism. "The compassion of God," writes Rabbi Dresner, "points the 'way' for man, for when a man acts compassionately, he is walking in the 'way' of the Lord. That is the meaning of *imitatio Dei.* "[23] Dresner observes that "the Law reared one to know the meaning of compassion; it commanded it, required it, taught it."[24]

Christian theology, which drew upon Greek thought, did not develop the doctrine of God in the light of the Hebrew awareness of God's compassion. All the more remarkable, therefore, is the reference of the Council of Toledo in 675: "It must be held that the Son was created, neither out of nothingness nor yet out of any substance, but that He was begotten or born out of the Father's womb *(de utero Patris),* that is, out of his very essence." Moltmann remarks that "whatever may be said about God's gynaecology according to this explanation, the point of these bi-sexual statements about the trinitarian Father is the radical rejection of monotheism, which is always patriarchal."[25] Trinitarian thinking of God, however, understands God relationally—that is, historically and dynamically out of a center in incarnation and atonement.

Knowing God in Jesus Christ

While it is clear that, for Christians at least, God is only fully revealed in Jesus of Nazareth, the God who was incarnate remains still the God of Israel, the God to whom the Old Testament gives witness. There cannot be any dualism at this point, as if there are to be two Gods, the God of Israel and the God who was incarnate in Jesus Christ. The God whom we have seen to be a suffering and compassionate God in dealings with Israel is the God now fully and uniquely revealed in Jesus.

In this section, we will take the inquiry forward by exploring what the history of Jesus means for our understanding of the suffering of God. Instead of seeking to understand who Jesus is in light of a prior philosophical understanding of God, as theologians have traditionally done, we will reverse the procedure. We will seek to understand God more fully in the light of Jesus Christ. In doing this we will arrive at an understanding of God quite different from the understanding of God found in classical theism. Thinking of God from a center in the incarnation reveals in a total way the God who is, of course, the suffering, compassionate God whom we found in the Old Testament.

While the philosophical tradition of God's lack of capacity for change and suffering teaches that God is not moved by any cause other than a cause within God, that cannot be the whole story as far as Christian faith is concerned. Building on the theological premise that God's true self or identity is revealed in Jesus Christ—that is, when we look at Jesus we see the face of God—we must begin to fill out our understanding of God in christological terms. God is in God's own being what God is toward us in the incarnate Jesus Christ. In the man Jesus of Nazareth we see and hear God in the fullness and truth of divinity come into the world. The Son of God, without ceasing to be God, subjected himself fully to the contingencies of historical existence (Phil. 2:5–11). The decisive point, as Thomas F. Torrance calls it, "is that in Jesus Christ it is God himself who has come among us savingly to make our existence and hurt his own, without ceasing to be what he is in his eternal reality."[26] In this case, knowledge of God is given on the basis of God's self-revealing in Jesus of Nazareth. Jesus' story is also God's story; God's story is also Jesus' story.

The very integrity and the credibility of the gospel are at stake here. The question of God's capacity for suffering is the question of the reality of the incarnation. If God truly assumed our humanity in Jesus Christ, and thereby penetrated into the depths of our human being, God must be understood in some way to be a God who has suffered. The incarnation demands this conclusion. If God is not capable of suffering, God has not really entered into history and taken on our flesh in a full way. As Torrance notes, "The God who has revealed Himself in Jesus Christ

as sharing our lot is the God who is really free to make
Himself poor, that we through His poverty might be made
rich, the God invariant in love but not impassible, constant
in faithfulness but not immutable."[27]

 Eberhard Jüngel notes that Christian theology has often
thought of God in such a way that it did not think of God
simultaneously as the God who was crucified.[28] This, as we
have already noted, meant that classical theology inserted
a huge gulf between God and Jesus as far as Jesus' suffering
was concerned. It meant too that in the suffering of Jesus,
God had not really shared our human lot. This conclusion
clearly makes nonsense of the incarnation and of the traditional teaching that Jesus, while having a divine and a
human nature, was one person.

 Earlier in his book Jüngel made the programmatic statement that "for responsible Christian usage of the word
'God,' the Crucified One is virtually the real definition of
what is meant with the word 'God.' Christian theology is
therefore fundamentally the theology of the Crucified
One."[29] This is an approach to the doctrine of God in
which we think about God out of a center in the cross of
Christ. This way of thinking leads irresistibly to a doctrine
of God's suffering and of God's capacity, therefore, for
compassion. While there are limitations to this approach,
and especially we note the danger of collapsing the incarnation into the cross, it is an approach in which we see the
emergence of a specifically Christian theology of God. The
cross of Jesus is not necessarily the only place at which to
begin the exploration of the doctrine of God christologically, but it is surely one of the places.

 As we have seen, then, it is vital to the integrity and
rationality of Christian faith that we assert that God was
fully and personally present in human history in all aspects
of the life and death of Jesus of Nazareth. The suffering
and death of Jesus mean then that God has taken suffering
and death into God's own experience. If this were not the
case, the passion was a fraud, a superficial event in which
God was not really involved but remained an unaffected
spectator. But because the Christ event was a God event

it is now a part of the history of God, a part of God's trinitarian life.[30] In other words, the incarnation and the cross force us to think about internal relations within God: that is, about the doctrine of the Trinity.

This trinitarian dimension has been memorably expounded by Jürgen Moltmann in *The Crucified God.*

> In the forsakenness of the Son the Father also forsakes himself. In the surrender of the Son the Father also surrenders himself, though not in the same way. . . . The suffering and dying of the Son, forsaken by the Father, is a different kind of suffering from the suffering of the Father in the death of the Son. . . . To understand what happened between Jesus and his God and Father on the cross, it is necessary to talk in trinitarian terms. The Son suffers dying, the Father suffers the death of the Son. . . . The Fatherlessness of the Son is matched by the Sonlessness of the Father, and if God has constituted himself as the Father of Jesus Christ, then he also suffers the death of his Fatherhood in the death of the Son.[31]

The death of Jesus, in other words, is now part of the history between the Father and the Son.

This has to mean that God, as Father and as Son, has been changed for all time by the cross of Jesus. God has been affected, acted on, by events in human history. According to Moltmann, it is precisely this trinitarian history of God implied in the suffering and death of Jesus Christ which liberates the concept of God from speculative theism and leads to a revolution in the concept of God.[32] God and suffering are not in contradiction to each other. On christological grounds it is necessary to say that suffering, dying, and death are a part of the experience of God. God has been forever changed by Jesus' incarnation into the vulnerability and contingency of the human condition.

The Compassionate God

It is one thing to speak of the suffering of God in the divine relationship with Israel and in the life and passion of Jesus Christ; it is something else to go on to say that God suffers because of us, or with us, or for us day by day. In other words, how do we speak of God continuing to be a suffering God? The issue here is primarily pastoral, concerned with knowing who God is today in relationship with us. A number of the theologies of the suffering of God leave us with the impression that God certainly suffered in the past. But it remains unclear how God participates redemptively in our suffering today. There is often little discussion of the relation between the great redemptive events of the past and the present experience of God with people in their ordinary lives and sufferings. In order to address this issue, we must move from the theology of the suffering of God to a consideration of the theology of the compassion of God. We are required to make the revolution in the concept of God even more thoroughgoing.

As we have seen, Jesus was a compassionate person. Compassion marked his ministry in a unique way. In the New Testament, only Jesus is spoken of as being compassionate. Used as a verb, the word is used only of Jesus. In other words, compassion functions as a theological word, referring to his messianic identity. Köster put it well: "The verb *splanchnizomai* has become solely and simply an attribute of the divine dealings."[33] The compassion of Jesus tells us something about God and about how God deals with us in our suffering. In order now to think theologically about the compassion of God, it is necessary to explore more fully the doctrine of the Trinity.

The doctrine of the Trinity is the attempt by the church to speak about God in terms both of God's indivisible unity and yet of the three distinct and personal modes of God's being. God is one God, yet God is also, traditionally, Father, Son, and Holy Spirit. Trinity, in other words, is another way of saying that there is relatedness within the unity of God. Although God is one, in the mystery of God's being there are internal relations within the Godhead. But how are we to understand this relatedness? How do the Persons of the Trinity "live together," so to speak?[34]

As we have argued, God is within God's own being what

God is toward us in Jesus Christ. Consequently, it follows that, as Jesus was compassionate, so too we must go on to say that God is compassionate. The statement about God's compassion, therefore, is not only a statement about God's way of being related to creation; it is a statement about God's way of being related to God, if we can speak that way. It is a statement about the internal relations within God, a statement about the Trinity. Compassion must be understood to express something of what we mean by divinity in that it refers us directly to the Trinity. Compassion expresses, in some way, how God is God.

Because God is compassionate, the Persons of the Trinity have to be understood in terms of a profound interaffectivity. The Persons are both open to one another and affected by one another. They are not isolated units of divine being. Perhaps we can say that the unity of the Godhead lies precisely in the supreme interrelatedness of the Persons. God's unity is constituted by this dynamic, relational identity. The Persons of the Trinity enter fully into one another's living space, as it were, feeling with one another the consequences of God's relatedness to creation. Compassion, then, is a part of God's Godness.

So far in this discussion we have moved from the consideration of God's act in Jesus to a consideration of God's being in God's internal trinitarian relations. It is also necessary now to look at this theological relation from the other direction, to go on to say, therefore, that who God was in Jesus Christ, as the Compassionate One, has its ground in who God is eternally as God, in God's own being as compassionate. God did not just become compassionate in the compassion of Jesus, as if prior to the incarnation compassion was not a part of God's being. The revelation of God to Israel makes clear that God was compassionate from the beginning of the divine history with humankind. But that, too, has its ground in the anterior fact of God's eternal compassion.

Understanding compassion in this way, moving now from the being to the act of God in Jesus Christ, has major significance for our understanding of God's way of being in relation with us today. God was not just compassionate in Jesus of Nazareth and then perhaps (who knows?) stopped being compassionate. Compassion cannot be relegated to be a purely past, historical, or even capricious aspect of God's dealing with us. Rather, compassion is to be seen as an irreducible attribute of God's divinity and therefore as an integral part both of God's ongoing way of relating to creation from the foundation of the world and of God's way of being within the Godhead. God will always act with compassion toward the world because, in doing otherwise, God would cease to be God, and that, clearly, is a nonsensical possibility. God, in other words, is unchanging—immutable, if you will—in God's self-willed desire to be and to continue to be compassionate. God is eternally compassionate. Compassion is a part of the being of God. This means that God will be compassionate in the future as God has been compassionate in the past.

Let us interject a critical question at this point. In reaction to the philosophical concepts of God's immutability and impassibility, are we not now in danger of collapsing the totality of the doctrine of God into compassion and thereby losing important aspects of God's stability as they are represented by traditional theology? If we say that God is compassionate—that is, that God is supremely suffering with and being changed by all that happens in the world—are we not now treading too near to the edge of reductionism? On the face of it, compassion increases the complexity of our understanding of God, for it demands a God who is in relationship with all of creation all of the time. But is there not more to God than this kind of supreme relatedness? While it seems to be theologically appropriate and necessary to speak of the compassionate God, of a profoundly, astonishingly affected and therefore changing God, are there not other aspects of God's being, of God's eternity, of God's transcendence, which we must be careful not to sweep away? Is there more to God than compassion, what is the nature of that "more," and how is it related to God's compassion?

A number of attempts at reconstructive theology in the light of the suffering of God have tried to solve this problem of holding together the aseity, or independence of God, and God's supreme relatedness. Abraham Heschel, for example, argued for a bipolar theology in which God as God is free yet able, through the divine pathos, to experience and be changed by the sufferings of the people. God is God of gods, yet also the God of the covenant with Israel. Commenting on Heschel, Moltmann notes that "the experience of the divine pathos inevitably leads to the perception of the self-differentiation of the one God."[35]

Heschel's view is similar to that advocated by the Danish Bishop Martinsen who, in a book translated into English in 1866, argued that God has a twofold life. God has a private life, as God of unclouded peace and self-satisfaction, and a life with the creation, to which the biblical writers refer when they speak of the divine grief and other feelings. "We may therefore say with the old theosophic writers, 'in the Outer Chambers is sadness, but in the inner ones unmixed joy.' "[36]

A contemporary attempt to address the same problem has been made by the process theologians, who take their lead from the organic metaphysics of Alfred North Whitehead. The process model is very complex, with its own language to describe both the internal relations within God and God's way of being supremely related to the world. There, too, we find a self-differentiation within God by which God relates totally to all feeling in the world, takes these feelings into the Godhead, and, through God's grasp of all possibilities, offers back to the world a lure, a new way of being, which if accepted will allow for movement toward greater fulfillment. The self-differentiation of God in process theology allows God to feel all feeling and know all possibilities, while retaining the notion of God's independence.

These examples of attempts at theological reconstruction illustrate how some theologians have grappled with the problem of holding together God's aseity, God's consistency, and God's relativity. Just to say that God suffers does not necessarily entail the collapsing of the doctrine of God into the suffering of God without remainder.

We come now to the heart of the doctrine of the compassion of God, to speak of God's way of being compassionate toward us day by day and to suggest how God's compassion relates to God's aseity. It is necessary here to develop a two-stage approach to our problem. On the one hand, we must retain the theological notion of the supreme interaffectivity of God. God as Trinity has compassion as the way in which the Persons "live together" within the Godhead. On the other hand, we must also retain the theological notion that Jesus Christ is the incarnation of the compassion of God in time and space. Jesus Christ is the Compassionate One. He is the full presence of God's compassion in history.

It is through Jesus Christ that God ministers to the needs of the world in compassion. Jesus "suffers with" the world, taking its suffering into himself, healing, renewing, saving, and comforting. That is his task. Because we are forced to think now in trinitarian terms, we can go on to say that God, whom Jesus called Father, in turn suffers with the "suffering with" of the Son, because the internal relations within the Trinity are characterized by compassion. In other words, God, in God's being as the first person of the Trinity, "suffers with" the suffering of the world by "suffering with" the "suffering with" of the Son. This first person of the Trinity shares in the Son's compassion through the compassion that characterizes the interior life of the Trinity.

Understood in this way, we are able to assert that God is compassionate both within the internal relations between the persons of the Trinity and in God's relations with the world through Jesus Christ. We are able to assert, further, that as Jesus is the focus of the compassion of the One whom he called Father, his Father experiences the world christologically, as it were, and not directly. In such a way we are able to speak intelligibly of the supreme relativity of God in Jesus Christ, by which God is compassionate, and still retain something of the insight of the classical doctrine in which God's eternity and independence have meaning in the first person of the Godhead. In this we steer clear of the heretical doctrine of patripassianism, condemned in the third century, which states that the Father suffers in the same way as the Son. Here, too, we have a model in which there is self-differentiation within God, although it is understood explicitly in relational trinitarian terms.

Is the compassionate God powerless? Or, to put the question differently, what, after all is said, is the point of God's suffering with us? Does it change anything? Compassion, as we saw earlier, always involves ministry. Jesus is never described as feeling compassion unless he goes on to do acts of healing, teaching, or feeding. It remains finally to explore how the theology of the compassionate God unfolds itself as the theology of the ministering God.

Compassionate ministry is Christ's ministry of faithfulness to the Father in the power of the Spirit on behalf of the world. The Holy Spirit continues this ministry, the Spirit that proceeds from the Father and the Son. This is not a new ministry, somehow different from Christ's ministry. It is the one ministry, which has its source in the life of the Trinity. As Ray S. Anderson observes, "This means that the world does not set the agenda for ministry, but the Father, who loves the world and seeks its good, sets the agenda. This christological, and actually Trinitarian, basis for ministry rules out both utilitarianism, which tends to create ministry out of needs, and pragmatism, which transforms ministry into marketing strategy."[37]

God's ministry of compassion in and through Jesus Christ is a ministry that is accomplished first of all in the completed work of Jesus Christ. Here we think of the work of atonement, in which God in Christ went all the way into our lostness and separation from God in order to restore us to relationship with God. God in Christ, in Christ's compassionate at-one-ment with us, entered into the depths of our sin and, in becoming as we are, enabled us to become as he is. The compassion of God allows us to catch a glimpse of the cost of atonement to God. Karl Barth notes that "what it means is that the suffering and sin and abandonment and peril of these men (who were like sheep without a shepherd) not merely went to the heart of Jesus but right into His heart, into Himself, so that their plight was now his own, and as such He saw and suffered it more keenly than they did."[38] We have noted already the cost of atonement in the parable of the compassionate father at Luke 15:11–32.

God's ministry of compassion is being accomplished, second, through God's continuing work in and through the Holy Spirit. God's ministry of compassion, of at-one-ment, continues as the Spirit's work within and among us. Even when we flee to the ends of the earth or make our beds in the place of the dead, even there God will meet us and hold us fast (Ps. 139). God's compassion is not a divine narcotic taking our suffering away. Rather, in compassion God continues to enter into the brokenness of our existence, to make the divine home there and to be our friend and companion who walks with us through the dark valley. To bring to mind again an image from Nicholas Wolterstorff, God sits beside us on our mourning bench.

A staggering contemporary statement of the compassion of God was written by Elie Wiesel, a survivor of Auschwitz and Buchenwald. The account, which describes the execution of two men and a boy, takes us into the heart of the compassion of God.

> The SS seemed more preoccupied, more disturbed than usual. To hang a young boy in front of thousands of spectators was no light matter. The head of the camp read the verdict. All eyes were on the child. He was lividly pale, almost calm, biting his lips. . . . The three victims mounted together onto the chairs. The three necks were placed at the same moment within the nooses. "Long live liberty!" cried the two adults. But the child was silent. "Where is God? Where is He?" someone behind me asked. At a sign from the head of the camp, the three chairs tipped over. . . . Then

the march past began. The two adults were no longer
alive. . . . But the third rope was still moving; being so
light the child was still alive. . . . Behind me, I heard the
same man asking: "Where is God now?" And I heard
a voice within me answer him: "Where is He? Here He
is—He is hanging here on this gallows."[39]

Compassionate ministry is not the actualizing of possibilities which exist somehow because of the gospel. Compassion is not a strategy or a program or—even less so—a
technique to be learned and applied. Rather, because
compassion exists as Christ's completed and continuing
ministry in the power of the Spirit, it is already both possible and actual. In which case, the task of the church is
determined by the ministry of Jesus Christ which has already gone before it and which continues to occur beyond
it. That ministry, however, is disclosed to us in the power
of the Holy Spirit (John 16:12–15). This means that the
church is faced with responsibility to discern the movement of God's continuing compassion in Jesus Christ and
seek ever and again to conform its own ministry to it. Only
in that way can the church's ministry of compassion be a
participation in Christ's continuing ministry of compassion. Only in that way, in fact, is compassion a possibility
for the church.

4

A Theology
of Compassionate Suffering

We now turn a corner in this study. Up to this point the focus of attention has been on Jesus, the Compassionate One, and on the significance of Jesus' compassion for our understanding of God. This was necessary in order to understand compassion on its own terms: that is, theologically. For the remainder of this study the focus of attention will be directed onto ourselves as we explore what it means for us to be compassionate persons.

The question now is, How can we become compassionate persons and what does compassion involve for us? The answer to this question is not as obvious as one might suppose.

As we have already seen, compassion is entirely a messianic reality. Jesus alone is the compassionate person, the one in whom compassion is an actuality. This means that compassionate ministry is possible for us only if we are in a relationship with Jesus Christ. Through our relationship with him we participate in his compassion. Our compassion, or, more accurately, his compassion in which we participate, is an expression of our life in Christ, the result of having died and risen with Christ (2 Cor. 4:10), of having been born again (John 3:3), of having been transformed by the renewal of our minds (Rom. 12:2). We recognize that apart from him we can do nothing (John 15:5).

Three areas need to be explored. (1) How might we understand the suffering that is necessarily involved in compassion, and what problems does that suffering pose for the continued possibility of compassion? (2) What is the process by which we live into our identity in Jesus Christ and thereby participate in his compassion? (3) What does participation in Jesus' compassion mean for ministry in practical terms? The following chapters will discuss the problems suffering poses for our continued compassion, the spirituality for compassion, and the ministry of compassion, respectively.

The Problem of Suffering

Suffering can cripple us. No matter how sound our theology is, or how intense we make our piety, or how firm our faith remains in spite of real difficulties, suffering can squeeze us dry. Suffering can come in many forms—political oppression, hunger, sickness, relationships breaking down, fear, meaninglessness, failure, bereavement, and others. But whatever its form, if it comes with sufficient intensity, suffering can destroy us as lively human beings. It can cut the ground out from under our feet, leaving us with no foundation for living. And nothing is gained by a sentimental assessment of suffering, especially when that assessment is given by one for whom much of the suffering in the world is a remote, unimaginable reality.

Compassion involves suffering. There is no way around the blunt fact that compassion will increase our experience of suffering. To suffer with another is still to suffer, even if we do not suffer another's suffering as he or she does. What is to prevent us from being squeezed dry? Left to itself, suffering, even in the most noble of causes, can cripple us as we buckle under the weight of accumulated pain. It is in this sense that we can properly speak of compassion as being potentially destructive.

When we buckle under the weight of unhealed suffering, compassion will inevitably get squeezed out to the margins of ministry. It is just too painful to continue as before. Compassion as an ongoing expression of appropriate Christian service is more than a matter of getting the theology of ministry right. It is more than the result of strong faith, vigorous piety, and hard work. The ongoing possibility of compassion as a part of our continuing life in and through Jesus Christ for the world is related directly to the possibility of the healing of our own suffering. Or, if not healing as such, then at least we must find ourselves in the process of being healed. We have to live the theological reality of new life in Christ in such a way that we are always ourselves being healed. Either we are being healed of our own suffering or compassion will become increasingly impossible for us.

The understanding of suffering requires some subtlety. Obviously, there are psychological and philosophical dimensions to the understanding of suffering. Pain is a part of the experience of life. But while pain is something we share with all living creatures, suffering involves a degree of self-awareness in which questions of ultimate meaning inevitably arise. Even more important, however, suffering has a theological dimension for persons of faith in which we seek to understand and, indeed, experience our suffering out of a center in God. It is the theological dimension that gives suffering an ultimate reference without which it would at best have only limited—that is, existential— meaning. Faith anchors the understanding and experience of suffering in God.

Although we must strive to understand suffering, and especially to understand it theologically, we ought not to speak glibly of this process of understanding for fear of missing something of its mystery and ambivalence. In many cases suffering is experienced as irrational, quite beyond any psychological, philosophical, or theological meaning, and therefore beyond understanding in any conventional sense. The Holocaust would be a case in point. In the face of such suffering all thought breaks apart. There is an appropriate speechlessness. To speak then of understanding suffering could be to minimalize or trivialize it or, worse, to make its unintelligibility banal or meaningless. We must beware of robbing suffering of its mystery. Suffering is much more than a problem to be solved.

Part of the mystery of suffering is that suffering is multifaceted. People suffer in a myriad different ways. And each person's suffering is unique to him or her, for truly we each experience only our own suffering. The sentence "I know how you feel" is nonsensical. It is also offensive. Suffering is incomparable. It is morally specious to qualify or quantify someone else's suffering. What is easy for one person to bear may be quite destructive for another. While one person may find profound meaning in his or her suffering, another may be plunged into the depths of despair and hopelessness. The meaning one person finds amid suffering may produce mind-numbing antipathy in another. For just as we cannot really experience another's suffering, neither can we find the same meaning in our suffering as is found by another in his or her suffering. Suffering, and what we do with it, is a road which, to some extent at least, each of us must travel alone. No matter the quality of help available, no matter the compassion of one's companions, suffering particularizes us. There is no single understanding of suffering; neither is there a single cure.

Apathy, a Response to Suffering

Earlier we made the statement that suffering, if it comes in sufficient intensity and remains unhealed, can cripple our capacity for compassion. Let us now look at that process more fully.

Our natural response to suffering in others and in ourselves is to turn away from it in some way. Our instinct is to avoid suffering if at all possible. There is a good reason for this. The sufferings of others, like our own sufferings, remind us of our vulnerability and mortality, and that is a most unpleasant reminder for most of us. "Underlying all suffering," writes Arthur C. McGill, "is the fact that human beings are needy. They do not have the sources for their strength and life within themselves."[1] Suffering brings us up against our limits. We come face-to-face with our personal contingency.

Persons whose curiosity is aroused by suffering and who seem attracted by it are plainly unhealthy. McNeill, Morrison, and Nouwen remark that "we do not aspire to suffer with others. On the contrary, we develop methods and techniques that allow us to stay away from pain." The call to compassion, in this case, "is a call that goes right against the grain."[2] Kazoh Kitamori, the Japanese theologian, remarks bluntly that "truly to weep with those who weep, to feel another's pain as intensely as one does one's own, is *psychologically* impossible."[3] We avoid suffering because the suffering of others is painful for us.

The psychological mechanism by which we avoid the full impact of suffering is very significant for our study of compassion. Apathy is a psychological resource by which we are able to avoid feeling some of the pain of life. Given that suffering, either another's or our own, is a part of our experience, apathy functions as a kind of buffer to keep us from feeling its full effects. Psychologically, apathy is a process of deadening the mind so that one no longer fully feels the negative or painful feelings that might threaten to be overwhelming. It results in psychic numbness, as if the emotional shut-off valve has been closed. The flow of affect stops. The psyche is frozen. Sensibility and awareness are significantly lowered. In other words, apathy serves as a form of psychological self-protection in the face of significant negative stimulation.[4] In this sense apathy can be viewed as a positive psychological resource. It functions to help us to survive when suffering threatens to overwhelm us. But there is a cost to pay: numbness, denial, indifference, lack of awareness, lassitude, depression.

Studies have shown that apathy was one resource which helped some people to survive the Nazi concentration camps and the aftermath of the Allies' dropping of atomic bombs during the Second World War. Knowledge was severed from feeling.[5] But we do not have to go to extremes in order to find apathy used as a resource to help people to cope with suffering. To a significant extent, apathy is an everyday experience used by all of us to block out or control negative stimulation. Indeed, it may be rightly supposed that to some extent apathy is necessary for mental health. As the information age presses in on us with increasing aggression, for example, who among us does not become apathetic in order to resist the avalanche of data that is quite beyond our digestion? Apathy acts here to help us to maintain some semblance of control over our lives. Or who, in the face of the visual bombardment of dead, dying, starving, or wounded people on our television screens night after night, does not mentally switch off, no longer being affected by the images and what they represent?

It is also appropriate to notice the role that apathy plays in certain professions. Could the medical, psychotherapeutic, or legal practitioner fulfill his or her professional responsibilities without a measure of apathy? Usually cosmeticized as "clinical distance," it is apathy nevertheless. And clearly this controlled apathy is deemed correctly to be a professional resource that allows the practitioner to get close enough to persons in need without being overwhelmed by that need.

Or reflect on the supermarket checkout clerk in an inner-city store standing hour after hour ringing up the purchases of strangers. The pain of boredom, meaninglessness, and alienation is lowered to a tolerable level by a studied nonrelating. We can see this same nonrelating apathy written on the faces of the commuters any morning or evening on the public transport vehicles in our large cities.

Clearly there is a question of degree to consider here. Our concern is with the slide toward the progressive blunting of the experience of suffering. The problem arises when, for any person or for the healing professional, apathy becomes not just a way of coping with excessive suffering, so that objectivity and judgment will not be impaired, but a way of life. When technique, technology, and distancing replace relationships, the patient or client (notice how one comfortably slips into the use of neuter objectifying labels) begins to feel like "the gallbladder down the hall" or "the hernia on the X-ray table." The client feels that he or she is of little personal significance for the practitioner. Apathy, in this case, is no longer a careful therapeutic device; it has become a defensive way of nonrelating in all professional circumstances. When apathy becomes a way of life, it keeps people at bay in spite of the professional commitment to help. Compassion is no longer possible. And healing is fundamentally compromised because the person is reduced to a complaint or condition.

While apathy has a healthy, even life-affirming side to it, some observers see apathy becoming today such a dominant psychosocial characteristic that they speak of an apathetic society. Such a society, in which apathy has become dominant, is schizoid, a society characterized by emotional coldness (or emotion reduced to sentimentality), aloofness, and a sense of superiority and detachment.[6] A schizoid society is a society in which people are no longer able to feel their own pain.

"Apathy," comments Dorothee Soelle, "is a form of the inability to suffer. It is understood as a social condition in which people are so dominated by the goal of avoiding suffering that it becomes a goal to avoid human relationships and contacts altogether. . . . Without question this ideal bears the imprint of middle-class consciousness."[7] Soelle's theological observations on apathy become sociocritical in nature as she locates one source of apathy in the consciousness of the satiated. As needs become satisfied and people no longer experience elementary forms of deprivation, their private prosperity blunts their awareness of the suffering of others. Personal property obscures public poverty and helps to cover up suffering.[8] Extending the analysis of the individual to the analysis of the society, Soelle maintains that society has become organized around the blunting of suffering. It is not that people do not suffer, of course, it is that in the officially optimistic society suffering is denied and repressed. It is hidden away from public view. People experience suffering, but it remains unnamed and unowned. It produces social numbness and blindness. A banal optimism prevails, Soelle maintains, built on the assumption that people do not suffer.[9] Walter Brueggemann's analysis of what he calls "the royal consciousness" makes a similar point about the social dimensions of apathy. By the royal consciousness he means the integrating synthesis of social policy and religion that serves to maintain the status quo. It is characterized by the economics of affluence, the politics of oppression, and a religion of immanence wherein God's over-againstness is dissipated. The royal consciousness, Brueggemann maintains, leads to the increase of satiation and the elimination of passion. "The royal consciousness with its program of achievable satiation has redefined our notions of humanness and it has done that to all of us. It has created a subjective consciousness concerned only with self-satisfaction. It has denied the legitimacy of tradition that requires us to remember, of authority that expects us to answer, and of community that calls us to care."[10] The royal consciousness in other words, the consciousness Brueggemann believes is characteristic of our society, "leads people to numbness, especially to numbness about death."[11]

We saw an example of the royal consciousness in the official publicity surrounding the colon cancer of President Ronald Reagan. In the days immediately preceding his surgery, the administration gave little indication that the problem was serious. The official optimism was carefully maintained. In the immediate and surely painful aftermath of surgery we saw photographs of a jaunty Mr. Reagan, waving, walking, and smiling as if nothing much was wrong. The President's cancer was transformed into a dazzling political success. He was packaged as a man who had barely suffered. While we admire his personal courage and strong human spirit amid personal adversity, he was packaged not as a vulnerable human being but as the icon of the officially optimistic society in which suffering must be suppressed or denied.[12]

One of Soelle's most helpful contributions to the discussion of apathy and suffering is her insight into suffering and language. "Extreme suffering," she notes, "turns a person in on himself completely; it destroys his ability to communicate." Suffering has the capacity to make us mute. "We are stripped of the autonomy to think, speak, and act."[13] Objectives cannot be organized. Behavior is reactive. One feels dominated by the situation, submissive and, above all, powerless.[14]

According to Soelle the movement away from apathy to a healthy response to suffering comes with speech. "The first step towards overcoming suffering is, then, to find a language that leads out of the uncomprehended suffering that makes one mute, a language of lament, of crying, of pain, a language that at least says what the situation is."[15] Bringing the suffering to articulation leads beyond apathy to an expression of suffering, which leads then to the third stage, that of confronting the situations which cause suffering in the first place. Speech is the prelude to political action. The critical stage in the healthy handling of suffering, in which one moves from reactive to proactive behavior, is the stage of lament, of articulation, in which suffering is expressed, in which it is named and owned. It is the indispensable step away from powerlessness and toward a sense of having some control over one's destiny.

Biblically, lamenting is an act of the community. Chapters 1, 2, 4, and 5 of the book of Lamentations, for example, are communal laments. "When biblical people wept, they wept with their friends," writes Eugene Peterson.[16] It is one of the tasks of compassion in the face of apathy, in the face of the denial of suffering and the absence of community, to transform what is private and individual and make it corporate and in some sense, therefore, public. Compassionate ministry must make lament possible for those who suffer in secret, and it must make lament corporate for those who suffer alone. Compassionate ministry has the responsibility of entering into the loneliness and aloneness of those who suffer. In compassion we recognize that shared—that is, expressed—pain is no longer as devitalizing and demobilizing as secret, private pain. As Henri Nouwen has noted, in words that have often been cited, "A minister is not a doctor whose primary task is to take away pain. Rather, he deepens the pain to a level where it can be shared."[17]

Compassion must have nothing to do with any strategy that circumnavigates lament. Religion which does that becomes a narcotic aiding in the denial or repression of suffering. Implicitly, that religion unwittingly aids the evil forces in the world which cause suffering. It is not adequate either to offer the power of positive thinking; that is a moral offense in the face of the suffering of millions upon millions of people today. There is more to human suffering than having a bad attitude toward unfortunate experiences. It is only when people are permitted to wail, like Rachel weeping for her children (Jer. 31:15 and Matt. 2:16–18), and are encouraged and accompanied in that wailing, that evil can be named for what it is and healing can begin. We agree with Soelle, who writes that "a religion deserves to be criticized radically when it claims to give people stability and yet doesn't even teach them to speak, thereby making them neurotic."[18]

We have spent some time exploring the nature of apathy because it is in the face of apathy in ourselves that compassion becomes less and less possible for us. While it is appropriate to speak of degrees of coping healthily with suffering, the logic of the conclusion is irresistible. If we are not able to feel our own suffering and consequently to utilize resources for healing, the possibility of compassion slips away from us. If I cannot feel my own suffering, there is no chance that I will be able to feel your suffering: that is, to suffer with you, to have compassion. In the light of this discussion of apathy, then, it is appropriate to suggest that apathy (a-pathos) is the opposite of compassion (com-pathos). The work of entering into the mystery of our own suffering, which is so necessary if we are to resist the corroding effects of deepening apathy, will need to be a significant part of the discussion of the spirituality of compassion in the next chapter.

What Makes Compassion Possible?

John le Carré, the English writer of espionage thrillers, has his hero, the aging spy George Smiley, pose a problem: " 'I have a theory which I suspect is rather immoral,' Smiley went on, more lightly. 'Each of us has only a quantum of compassion. That if we lavish our concern on every stray cat, we never get to the center of things. What do you think of it?' "[19] Smiley's theory reflects the message of the fairy story of the warm fuzzies and the cold pricklies. The wicked witch deceived the children into believing that if they gave away all their warm fuzzies, of which hitherto there had been an unlimited supply, they would soon run out. The witch scared the children into hoarding their warm fuzzies and even into giving cold pricklies disguised as warm fuzzies.

Is compassion a limited resource? No matter how well we deal with our suffering and resist the slide into apathy, does not experience in ministry teach us that there is only so much compassion that we are capable of? In discussions on the theme of compassion no other questions arise as frequently. There is significant pragmatic power in these questions. We all know what it is to reach the end of our tether. That we have limits is taken to be a matter of fact.

It is important to recognize and affirm that rest and recreation are as essential and legitimate parts of ministry as is action. We all must withdraw from the fray of ministry on a regular basis or else become beaten down by it. A practical theology of sabbath rest is something we need to recover again in our activistic contemporary Christianity.

But the problem over limits is yet more profound than the proper concern for rest. At bottom we are concerned about a theological understanding of the possibility of compassion. A proper response to the concern about limits must finally be dealt with on the basis of what makes compassion possible in the first place.

Alternative models of the Christian life and ministry can be derived from the parable of the good Samaritan. The first option erroneously reverses the fundamental theological order. It is very common, and although it is alarmingly destructive in its consequences, it still tends to dominate our thinking and skews our understanding of the limits of compassion. In diagrammatic form, it looks like this:

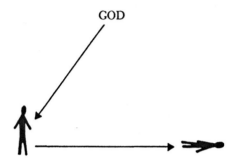

According to this interpretation of the parable, God charges a person to be compassionate and to go and pick up wounded people. It is assumed—and it is a fair assumption, up to a point—that those whom God calls God also empowers. The person then moves in obedience into a ministry of tending to wounded people (or any other ministry to which one believes oneself to be called). The model is fundamentally pragmatic. Once the call is recognized, the dominant question then becomes, How do I do ministry? It may be accurate to say that this model has dominated the training of the clergy during this century to some extent, at least, turning the seminary into a trade school.[20]

In support of the model, we affirm that it is concerned with ministry, and with the relationship between God and the person in ministry. But there is a cost. This understanding of ministry tends to set up a Ping-Pong match in which the ministering person bounces back and forth between two extremes. If he or she picks up every wounded traveler, exhaustion will soon set in, to be accompanied inevitably by anger, disillusionment, and despair. In other words, the minister will experience what we now call burnout. If, on the other hand, he or she does *not* pick up every wounded traveler, guilt will cripple his or her ministry every bit as quickly as exhaustion. This model of ministry leads, then, to a two-step dance as one beats a rhythm between burnout and guilt. Compassion cannot be understood as a human possibility waiting to be actualized. The result will always be either the limitation of compassion because of exhaustion or a lapse into apathy and guilt, which makes compassion impossible.

There is another way to understand ministry in the light of the parable of the good Samaritan, a way that is forced upon our understanding by the dogmatic reality of compassion itself. In this alternative understanding there is a change in the fundamental movement within the model, a change that illustrates how the Christian's compassionate ministry only arises out of our participation in God's ongoing ministry of compassion in the power of the Spirit.

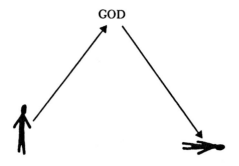

GOD

Here we see that God is the minister. In the New Testament, we must remember, compassion is a messianic designation, a capacity for ministry reserved only for Jesus. Only God in Christ can take on the suffering of the world in compassion and not be destroyed by it. Only God can heal the world's brokenness. All ministry is God's ministry, or, more accurately, God's ministry in Jesus Christ, to the glory of the Father, in the power of the Spirit, for the sake of the world.[21] Ministry is not a pragmatic attending to human need wherever that arises for us. Rather, ministry is first of all God's work of healing and saving in Jesus Christ, and our ministry finds its identity, goal, and possibility entirely from that actual prior ministry.

As we look at this second model, it is important to understand that we are, first of all, the persons lying in the ditch and in need of divine help. God in Christ ministers in compassion to us, taking the first step. It is because we have been incorporated into Christ by Christ's taking our wounded humanity upon himself, an event sealed by our baptism, that we are able then to participate in his ongoing life for the world. In practical terms, this means accepting our responsibility to attend to our relationship with Christ, a relationship established and maintained by him, recognizing that outside of that relationship we have no way of participating in God's ongoing ministry to the world (John 15:1–5). The Christian's ministry in general, and compassion in particular, as our participation in this divine ministry, flows out of our life in Christ. Our life in Christ and our work of ministry can never be separated in this case. Outside of our life in Christ, ministry really becomes impossible for us, for it becomes our ministry and not God's ministry in which we by grace participate. Spirituality and ministry always belong together.

Ministry is a way of being in relationship with Jesus Christ so that we participate in his life for the world. In fact, we cannot claim to be in relationship with Jesus Christ and not participate in his ministry for the sake of the world. Ministry is "through Jesus Christ," in the same way in which prayer and worship are "through Jesus Christ." As in prayer we pray through Jesus Christ, joining our prayers to his, and as we worship God through the Son, so also in ministry we live and work through Jesus Christ.

As this model has been shared with a number of groups, a question has often arisen: Should there not be a line along the bottom, connecting the ministering person and the wounded person? The problem with that question is that it still assumes we can relate to people otherwise than through Jesus Christ our Lord. To attempt to relate to others outside of our being in Christ would be to claim a false autonomy for ourselves, to act as if we were not in Christ and were not always and only related to all creation through Jesus Christ. To live and act in such a way is to live and act denying our baptism. It is to claim a false autonomy. Jesus Christ is the middle term connecting and binding the minister and the person ministered unto. In such a way, he is the sole mediator and minister between heaven and earth and between the individual members of his body.

The practical question for us to face now is, How do we live that theology? How do we live "in Christ" with respect to our own suffering and the suffering that increases for us in compassion? Or, to put the question the other way around, How does God in Christ heal us, thereby enabling us to be the compassionate persons God calls us to be? The questions concerning the limits of compassion are, at bottom, deeply theological and relate directly to the very practical issue of our life in Christ. We will conclude this chapter by looking at some of the theological concerns highlighted by this question, leaving the exploration of practical spirituality for the next chapter.

Suffering in Christ: A Theological Paradigm

Our task now is to explore a theological understanding of suffering and to see how God is involved in its healing or redemption. We will look first at biblical approaches to suffering in a broad way in order to get some sense of the wider picture. The final part of this section will be given over to the discussion of one major New Testament image: suffering in Christ.

Our understanding of suffering relates directly to our view of the world. If we see the world as a random event, suffering only has the meaning we choose to give it. There is no transcendent ground, nothing beyond personal or social experience and what we make of it. If, on the other hand, we see the world as having a ground in God, suffering must be understood in reference to that God. This raises the age-old problem of theodicy, of course: How can God be all-loving and all-knowing and yet still permit suffering? If disaster strikes, God's care, power, or goodness can be called into question. Or else we look for meaning precisely in God. This broadly is the approach to suffering that we find in the Bible. Suffering is dealt with by reference to God.

In the Old Testament all suffering is related ultimately to Yahweh in some way. Israel is Yahweh's possession, and any break in relationship with Yahweh inevitably leads to suffering of some kind. But this cannot be understood in a flat, causal, or one-dimensional way. The Deuteronomist, for example, writing during the exile, offers a fairly well-known theological scheme involving God's faithfulness, Israel's disobedience, God's anger, Israel's repentance, and God's mercy and blessing. Yet elsewhere the Old Testament speaks of the remoteness of God. Psalm 10, verses 1 and 11, suggests that God is off in the distance or simply forgetful or hiding so as not to see suffering. This leads to a prayerful pleading for God to arise and do something. There is a force to this pleading, an edge of immediacy, that contrasts with the high "classroom" theology of the Deuteronomist. Then again, God is sometimes seen to inflict arbitrary suffering on the innocent. This, of course, is Job's story. God holds the reins of life and death and is accountable to no one. The ultimate offense to natural moral reason, perhaps, is God's apparent willingness to let the godless prosper while the godly suffer all kinds of indignities.[22]

The Old Testament allows suffering to be suffering. It does not gloss over its pain or the theological problems it can pose. Suffering is real; it is not imaginary or an experience that is peripheral to a person in some way. The Old Testament refuses to spiritualize suffering. In fact, the Old Testament again and again gives expression to the cry of lament in the face of suffering, a cry that all too clearly shows the depth and reality of pain.

There is no single meaning given to suffering in the Old Testament. Sometimes it is seen as the result of evil deeds

boomeranging back upon a person (e.g., Prov. 26:27), or as
expiation whereby Israel's suffering moves God to modify
the people's fate (e.g., Ex. 3:7–8), or it is seen as punishment (e.g., Deut. 32:35) or discipline (e.g., Prov. 13:24), or
as a satanic counterthrust (e.g., Ps. 18:4–5), or even as the
inscrutable purpose of God (e.g., Jer. 10:23–24).[23] Whatever the particular point of reflection on the cause of suffering, the Old Testament always deals with suffering in
the context of faith in Yahweh. Somehow or other, God
was working out the divine purpose.

Suffering was dealt with in a number of different ways
in the Old Testament. Wisdom literature counseled the
avoidance of evil and a rational commonsense approach to
life. Ritual responses, prayers of imprecation, threats of
revenge, and the prophetic attack on suffering at its root
in spiritual and social evil all find a place in the Old Testament. Above all else, however, the Old Testament teaches
that God is involved intimately with the plight of the people. This is the basis for hope.

Jesus was not a theologian in the conventional sense. He
was more interested in doing something about suffering
than in interpreting its meaning. His life was lived struggling against suffering. Like the Old Testament, the New
Testament and, consequently, Christian faith take suffering very seriously indeed as a fact of faith and as a reality
to be countered.

The New Testament builds on the Old Testament. With
respect to suffering, the beginning and end of Jesus' life
reflect Old Testament themes: Matthew 2:17–18, for example, recalls Rachel weeping for her children, and the
passion narratives, of course, are replete with Hebrew
images. From the Old Testament, the church learned that
suffering was a mode of faith.[24] Like the Old Testament,
the New refused to spiritualize suffering or reduce it away
as somehow less than real. To do so would have been to
undercut the incarnation, the very source of the faith.
Jesus suffered, and in his suffering he entered into the
human condition in every way.

Like Judaism, Christianity is a religion of suffering. At its center we see Jesus, the crucified God. But Jesus' suffering was not regarded in the New Testament as a specific case of suffering in general. His suffering was unique. To suffer, *pascho* in the Greek New Testament, is used only of Jesus in the Synoptics. Jesus is the sufferer. His suffering defines our suffering. And his suffering allows us to be secure in the knowledge that God is a God who suffers. Because Jesus suffered as he did, and because he as God was wholly human, there is now no human suffering that is outside of his Lordship over suffering. For those who are baptized there can now be no private suffering or dying: "If we live, we live to the Lord, and if we die, we die to the Lord; so then, whether we live or whether we die, we are the Lord's" (Rom. 14:8). Suffering in Christ makes all human suffering a social experience (1 Cor. 12:26).

And if Jesus' life itself was characterized by suffering, likewise the Christian's life, a life in Christ, would consequently be characterized by suffering. For example, Mark 10:38–39 refers to drinking the cup Jesus drank and being baptized with the baptism he received. This language signifies shared suffering. Luke 14:27 refers to the Christian's own cross-bearing as a part of following Jesus. Luke 9:23 tells us that we must take up our cross *daily*. Suffering, it would seem, was understood by Jesus to be a constitutive part of discipleship. The Christian is called on to endure the same fate as Jesus at John 15:18. Servants are not greater than their master. If he is persecuted, they likewise will be persecuted (John 15:20). Philippians 1:29 teaches "for it has been granted to you that for the sake of Christ you should not only believe in him but also suffer for his sake." These and similar texts indicate that suffering was understood to be a part of living the gospel.

The gospel does not lead to a sentimentalization of suffering or to an experience of life as a despairing vale of tears. To participate in Christ's suffering is also to participate in Christ's life. In general terms the Christian hope is related directly to the resurrection of the body, and therefore to the coming future of the kingdom of God which is promised, announced, and anticipated. There is always the danger with this doctrine that it will function as a premature and inappropriate access point to heaven, allowing us to flee the earth while we still have work here to do. The well-known Marxist point about religion being the opiate of the people, the hope for freedom from suffering that takes people out of the world rather than leading people to transform the world, remains pertinent. But given New Testament faith, and Christianity at its best, that criticism does not address the reality. For true Christian hope sends us back into the world, to become historical in a wholly new and radical way as we announce and anticipate the kingdom of God which is promised.[25] The theology of hope leads to a prophetic energizing and criticizing of that which is not yet the kingdom, of those structures and conditions in society which lead to numbness, despair, and death. Hope also means that evil, suffering, and death do not have the last word.

In spite of the general fact that neither the Old nor the New Testaments have a single view of suffering and its healing, we are not left with an unedifying relativism on the matter. Although Paul's notion of suffering in Christ is, in one sense, just one image among many, it does seem to have a centrality which allows us to suggest that it takes us close to the heart of the matter. We will now discuss Paul's complex notion of suffering in Christ as a theological paradigm that helps us to understand how we can participate in Christ's compassion in an ongoing way.

There are a fairly large number of texts in which Paul writes of his own suffering or of human suffering in general in terms of faith in Jesus Christ (2 Cor. 1:3–9; 4:7–14; 7:3; 12:9; 13:4; 1 Thess. 1:5–8; 2:13–16; Rom. 8:17; Phil. 3:2–11). To these can be added a number of instances where Paul writes on similar or related themes, as, for example, our dying with Christ as the basis for new life. In all, there is substantial biblical literature on suffering and our faith in Christ.[26]

We will discuss one passage, 2 Corinthians 4:7–14, and draw conclusions from it. This passage presents the significant themes for our purpose. At verse 10 Paul refers to the death of Jesus and the life of Jesus as something in which he shares. This remarkable and complex notion means that Paul "interprets his suffering in terms of participation in Christ's death and resurrection."[27] What leads Paul to such an astonishing conclusion, and what does it mean for his understanding of suffering in practical terms?

The passage begins at verse 7 with the well-known statement concerning the truth of the gospel being contained in earthenware jars, mere bodies of clay. But this human weakness and vulnerability make it clear that the success or viability of Christian life does not depend upon our efforts but upon the overwhelming power of God. To put this in the language of the earlier parts of this chapter, Paul does not subscribe to the pragmatic model of ministry that leads only to guilt or burnout. Ministry is not a possibility waiting to be actualized on the basis of his efforts. Rather, it is the transcendent power of God that is the force for ministry. The possibility of ministry is derived from the actuality of God's power and ministry and of the Christian's participation in them through Jesus Christ.

Verses 8 and 9 describe, in a series of paired parallels that depend upon verse 7, the extent to which Paul is battered and bruised by ministry. He has had his difficulties, but he has never been beaten down by them. Sometimes he could not see his way through problems, but he has never despaired. He was persecuted but never deserted. He was physically abused but never killed. In spite of severe hardship, then, Paul has felt himself preserved by the power of God. However, the point is not just the contrast between suffering and preservation.

In verse 10, Paul relates his suffering to carrying in his body the death of Jesus. He has been baptized into Christ's death (Rom. 6:3). Robert C. Tannehill suggests that the death of Jesus is an active power at work in Paul's body (see verse 12). The continuing power of death does not mean that redemption is incomplete, however. Death has been destroyed, and it is now forced to take the role of the death of Jesus. Death stands now in a relation to power and life. "The power of the old dominion has been transformed into a power which serves the new dominion in its present form."[28] The life of Jesus corresponds to the power of God referred to at verse 7. What Paul is referring to here as the life of Jesus is nothing less than the resurrection life of Jesus. The connection between power and Jesus' resurrection is not unfamiliar in Paul's thought. Thus there are two realities at work in the Christian: the death of Jesus, which is his conquering of the power of death, and the life of Jesus, which is the power of God at work.

Verse 11 indicates what kind of experience Paul has in mind when he refers to the death of Jesus: we suffer "for the sake of Jesus." "For Paul the idea of participating in Jesus' death and resurrection is not a mere theological generality, but a means of understanding the particular experiences of his own life."[29] As long as he is dying or suffering for Jesus' sake, the life of Jesus is at work within and through him. This dying with Christ in Christian life is a daily experience and leads to life for the church (v. 12). Suffering is not good in itself, of course. But in the mystery of the gospel, God uses human suffering to grant life. This, says Tannehill, is something God does anew on each occasion, and so the Christian life carries within it the notion of expectation.[30]

That which enables Paul to carry on amid terrible hardship and suffering is derived entirely from God. Paul's references to his own weaknesses make clear that it is God's power which is at work and not his own (2 Cor. 12:9–10). For this reason, Paul does not see his suffering in a negative light. His suffering allows him to participate in the death of Jesus and therefore to share in his resurrection life. While Paul's present suffering, and indeed his dying, is certainly a sign of the continuing power of the old aeon, even more it is a sign of God's hidden victory over the power of death in Jesus Christ. God has usurped suffering and death and can use them now for God's own purposes. This is a paradox which we should probably say bursts thought apart, for it certainly cannot be explained.

It is a miracle, as verses 7 to 9 make clear. It is the revelation of God's power in situations of human impotence. God brings new life from death for the believer. This leads Paul away from all boasting, for in all things he has to rely entirely on God for the new life that is at work within him. Even his existence as an earthen vessel has a positive significance, for it serves to reveal the power of God. "In his sufferings Paul is constantly reminded of his own weakness. He is forced again and again to look away from himself to the power of God. Thus Paul's continuing participation in Christ's death through suffering maintains and affirms his past death with Christ, and so enables Paul to receive the new life which comes from God."[31]

A study of the other passages that refer to dying and rising with Christ in suffering would provide further elaboration, but we have now before us the essential argument: Christ is Lord of life and death; in our suffering and dying we participate in his Lordship over death and so his life and its power are at work within us. We do not suffer unto ourselves. Rather, the Christian's sufferings are now seen to have become Christ's sufferings. Understood now as suffering in Christ, our suffering announces the promise of life.

If the ministry of compassion is a participation in the ongoing compassion of Jesus Christ, as we have argued, it comes as no surprise to discover that suffering is also to be understood in the same way, as a participation in the suffering of Christ. In fact, to participate in Christ's suffering, and therefore to share in his life and power, is the counterpart of the participation in Christ's compassion. It is the one reality seen from two different points of view. This covers the "suffering with" of compassion in a wholly theological light. It is suffering, certainly, but it is now no longer seen to be just an autonomous negative experience. Although the suffering of compassion remains what it is, a painful, difficult, and possibly even deadly experience, it is even more so an intimation of new life, of life in Christ. This is not a mysticizing or spiritualizing of compassionate suffering, in which we pretend that it is less than it really is. It is rather an understanding of suffering as a theological event. In this case, suffering is not understood in its own terms, so to speak, but now as a relational reality, in terms of our life in God.

The material in this chapter cannot be left to stand alone. We have been concerned to make a theological probe toward understanding the suffering that compassion necessarily involves for the Christian and to explore the problems that emerge. It is necessary now to move from this rather abstract and complex discussion to look at the way in which someone would actually participate in Christ's compassion in practical terms. We turn our attention to the process by which we live into our compassionate identity in Jesus Christ. To put it in other language, our concern now is to develop a spirituality for compassion by which the issues discussed in this chapter may be explored and experienced in practical terms.

5

Living with the Wound
of Compassion

The vision at the heart of this inquiry is the belief that
compassion is rooted entirely in our relationship with
Jesus Christ, the Compassionate One. Our compassion is a
participation in his compassion. As we live ever more fully
into our true identity that lies hidden in Christ (Col. 3:3),
compassion increasingly becomes a part of our lives. Compassion is the overflow of our life in Christ. It is time now
to look at what this means in practical terms. How do we
grow in relationship with Jesus Christ? And what in particular is involved for us if we wish truly to participate in his
compassion? Our task is to develop a spirituality for compassion. Because compassion is the fruit of intimacy with
God, compassion and spirituality inevitably belong together.

Because our goal is to develop a spirituality for compassion, our focus is specific rather than general. Of course, to
be in relationship with Jesus Christ will always lead to
compassion, because compassion is a part of his being. Our
task, however, is not to attend to the broad sweep of
spirituality, to say all that can be said on the matter, but
to find assistance in the task of becoming compassionate.
What in particular do we have to attend to in our relationship with God in Christ in order that we may ever more
fully participate in Jesus' ongoing compassion for the
world?

Reclaiming Spirituality

Spirituality is a difficult word to define. Unfortunately it is a word trapped in narrow stereotypes that sometimes bear little relation to reality. For some people it conjures up negative images of a world-denying, apolitical, individualistic, and privatistic piety. Especially for Protestants, perhaps, the word conjures up aspects of Catholicism from which they are just as happy to maintain distance. Of course, there is no smoke without fire, and the stereotypes do have some basis in fact. The core model of the Christian life during many centuries may be characterized by the image of climbing Jacob's ladder, an image from which, unfortunately, Protestants have not been immune. The movement toward God was seen to be an ascent, and so hierarchy, individualism (only one person can be on a rung of the ladder at any one time), competitiveness, and a fleeing from the earth came to be seen as the spiritual tasks. One earned one's way up to God.[1]

Old models die hard, in spite of over four hundred years of Protestant theology to guide us. The Reformation stood the ladder model of spirituality on its head with its high doctrines of justification and sanctification, understood now as objective realities in Jesus Christ and not as tasks to be achieved by dint of human effort. The Christian life was to be understood entirely in terms of the efficacious, vicarious, objective work of Jesus Christ, in whom and through whom we are both made right with God and have holiness. It is precisely in the Reformation recovery of these classical doctrines that we have the basis for a theology of Christian spirituality which breaks free from the continuing influence of the old Catholic theology of climbing our way up to God.

Justification describes the action of God in Christ by which we are put into a right relationship with God. The heart of the gospel is the justification of the ungodly, of those who are separated from God. We stood judged and condemned. And there was nothing that we could do from our side of the divine-human relationship to restore ourselves to communion with God. But now we have been restored to fellowship with God through the atoning death of Jesus. He bore the cost of our alienation and separation from God. Justification describes our objective status before God as the result of the work of Jesus in his death: judged but acquitted, condemned but pardoned. It is the signature tune of redemption.

Because the Reformers could allow their thinking to be controlled by the life as well as the death of Jesus, the doctrine of justification, which relates to the work of his death, has, correspondingly, as its corollary the doctrine of sanctification, which relates to the work of his life. Jesus of Nazareth, from the side of creation, as a human person, offered his life as a totally loving and acceptable response to God. He was the righteous human person, the one who offered the obedient and filial life of worship, prayer, and ministry. He was the Holy One. As we are justified through his atoning death, so we are sanctified through his holy life. In him we are both made right with God and brought into intimacy with God. Jesus Christ is our salvation *and* our holiness. Justification and sanctification belong together as objective realities. They are done for us, and that is why they are good news. The ladder is well and truly abolished. Salvation and holiness now describe our true condition. This is our life hidden with Christ in God (Col. 3:3).

The image which fits better with Reformation theology is that of living into the life we have in Christ, into the holiness that is already ours in him. Rather than seeing the fledgling Christian beginning the climb to God from the bottom of the ladder, we may characterize the Reformers as arguing that the Christian begins at the top of the ladder because salvation in every sense is a completed reality in Jesus Christ. In Jesus Christ we are already in relationship with God in the fullest sense; we are saints of God. And because that is the case, we cannot slip back down the ladder; neither can we by our own efforts climb any higher. It is at this point, probably, that we would do well to dispense with ladder images altogether.

Spirituality as we understand it here is a perspective on

baptism. Baptism is the declaration that we belong to God and that our identity is in Christ. It is the sign of new personhood, of having died and risen with Christ. To be baptized means that we belong to Christ and have our existence now only as a part of his body. Baptism is the sign and seal of our new identity. To discover one's true self is to discover the truth of one's baptism.

In our sense of the term, spirituality in a practical sense refers first of all to the disciplined work of attending to our relationship with God in Christ. This is a relationship that is complete in Christ, as we have just seen. It defines who we are. It constitutes our personhood. Our identity is our identity in Jesus Christ: "I have been crucified with Christ; it is no longer I who live, but Christ who lives in me" (Gal. 2:20).

If salvation and holiness describe who we are in Christ, they hardly describe what we know of ourselves and what we see in others. We know only too well that we are broken people; the good we want to do, we do not do, and the evil we do not want to do, we find ourselves doing (Rom. 7:19). The question is, Will we live now into the holiness that defines objectively who we are already in Christ, or will we live a lie, as though we were not made holy in him? Will we live into the reality of our baptism, or will we live denying our baptism? Far too often we live a lie.

Thomas Merton, the late American Trappist monk, expressed the issue before us with characteristic insight:

> For me to be a saint means to be myself. Therefore the problem of sanctity and salvation is in fact the problem of finding out who I am and of discovering my true self. . . . We can be ourselves or not, as we please. We are at liberty to be real, or to be unreal. We may be true or false, the choice is ours. We may wear now one mask and now another, and never, if we so desire, appear with our own faces.[2]

We can choose to become laws unto ourselves if we wish; we can become self-justifying (self-righteous rather than righteous in Christ). But this is to restore the ladder back to its place of prominence. It is also idolatry.

There is, then, a gap between our being in Christ and our behavior. What we are in God's eyes in Jesus Christ is not always represented by what we are in practice or experience. In large measure spirituality is the work of closing that gap. This involves the letting go of a false autonomy and a coming to terms with both identity in and dependency upon God. This means a dying to oneself as an object of interest to find oneself more fully alive in Christ.[3] Living into our identity in Christ means prayer and Bible reading; it involves the ongoing struggle for honest repentance as we confess our willful separation from God; it obligates us to disciplines of worship and intimacy with God's people. It is by these tasks of obedience and discipline that we are opened little by little and can experience intimacy with God, with ourselves, and with one another. Spirituality involves placing ourselves before God day by day in order that we may come home to ourselves by accepting our true personhood. It means naming the lies by which we live and daring to cast aside the masks we use to hide our true identity from ourselves and from the outside world. Spirituality is the work of making holiness practical as we seek to live the truth of our identity in Christ. To cite Merton again, it means praying for our own discovery.[4]

Spirituality refers, second, to the consequence of living into our identity in Jesus Christ, the work of being more fully and more faithfully God's person in ministry to the world's pain. This distinguishes spirituality from what is conventionally taken to be the meaning of piety, a kind of purely privatized devotion. Spirituality has as its goal the living out of one's faith, one's identity, in the world. Compassion is one way in which that comes to historical expression. The devotional life does not stand by itself. Prayer is for ministry. A spirituality that does not lead us to become God's ministers in some way or another is not a spirituality rooted in the life of Jesus Christ, who came that all persons might have abundant life. We cannot claim to be in relationship with the incarnate world-affirming Lord and then, in his name, turn away from that same world as if it were unimportant. Spirituality is the basis for a profound and particular kind of worldliness, a worldliness arising out of the mission of the incarnation itself. To be in relationship with the world-affirming Lord of redemption is necessarily to be thrust into the world with ever-increasing commitment to his kingdom.

As we have defined it, spirituality has an inward and an outward dimension. They belong together as two parts of the whole. Intimacy with God, which inevitably leads to intimacy with our true selves, leads to intimacy with the world. The spiritual life is the life that is lived in the light of the movement between relationship with God in Jesus Christ and ministry. In this understanding, it is clear that spirituality does not call for a privatistic withdrawal from the world and its problems. On the contrary, spirituality calls us to a radical worldliness in which our task is no less than the transformation of the world for the glory of God. As we live ever more fully into our objective life in Christ, we become ever more faithfully God's persons in ministry to the world.

Disciplines for Compassion

Compassion is not a skill to be mastered. We cannot take compassion by storm. It is a way of life, a spirituality in the fullest sense. It is the reflection of that which constitutes our center, the living out of our true selves, our being in Jesus Christ. As McNeill, Morrison, and Nouwen note, "Compassion is not conquered but given, not the outcome of our hard work but the fruit of God's grace."[5]

To speak of compassion as a gracious or gifted way of life does not imply that we have no role to play in the process, however. The authors just cited go on to note that discipline is indispensable in the compassionate life. "Without discipline, the forces that call us by our old names and pull us into competitive games are too strong to resist. . . . We need a concrete and specific way that can provide formation, guidance, and practice. We need to know not only about the compassionate life but also about the compassionate way."[6]

Discipline is a resource by which we allow ourselves to attend to someone or something in an ongoing way. It is an attending that we will not allow to be deflected by passing whims or be betrayed by laziness. Discipline has resolve about it. But discipline is not an end in itself. Disciplines help us to get from here to there. They are means to ends that lie beyond the disciplines themselves. To put it in other language, disciplines are vehicles of grace that enable us to move toward a goal.

Everything important in our lives demands the care of discipline if that part of life is to remain nurtured and healthy. Relationships, for example, demand discipline. They take hard work, concentrated attention, and time-consuming commitment. If we cannot be bothered, the relationship will eventually show the consequence of poor maintenance. It is no different in our relationship with God. Our ancestors in the faith who walked closely with God knew this well. The saints call out to us through the mists of history; faithfulness demands discipline.

Theologically, spiritual disciplines can best be understood in terms of the old distinction between contracts and covenants. A contract is based on mutual and bilateral relationships. The parties to the contract have equal status before the law, and it takes the two parties to be in agreement before a binding contract exists. If one of the parties does not fulfill his or her part, the contract is broken and the aggrieved party may seek redress. When we understand spiritual disciplines in a contractual way, the interior life consists of obeying the imperatives of an agreed-upon arrangement. If we fulfill our side of the contract, all is well. If, however, we fail to say our prayers, then the wrath of heaven will be loosed upon us. Our Christian lives, our relationships with God, quickly become knotted with fear and guilt. We are likely to find ourselves giving up the spiritual life altogether.

God has not entered into a contractual relationship with

us. Rather, God has entered into a covenant with us, and it is out of this covenant that we can develop a theologically sound and psychologically healthy approach to spirituality. A covenant is a unilateral relationship, called into being by one party and maintained in existence by that party. There is nothing democratic about covenants. God, in unconditional election, has placed us in relationship. And nothing from our side can deflect God from covenantal faithfulness (see Rom. 8:38–39). While the covenant demands obligation, the continued existence of the covenant is not conditional upon it. God has chosen that it be that way, and we make a theological error of terrifying magnitude when we substitute the legal notion of contract for the gracious theological notion of covenant.

The covenantal indicative ("I love you and have claimed you from the foundation of the world through Jesus Christ") is prior to and makes possible the covenantal imperative ("Now, therefore, this is how you will act"). Holiness, if we can put it this way, is the gift and demand of God. But when we fail to meet the demand, as we will again and again, we are cast back upon the mercy and compassion of God which is in Jesus Christ. God remains faithful even when we are not. Make no mistake, the covenant makes unconditional demands upon us. We are called into intimate and obedient response. But this is not a contractual obligation that we must meet in fear. It is the gift and demand of love, but even in our failing we cannot void the covenant.

Spiritual disciplines allow us to place ourselves before God. In them we respond to the luring covenantal love of God, which seeks to bring us ever deeper into relationship with God. As we noted, the disciplines are not ends in themselves. They are steps toward deeper relationship by which we are able more fully and faithfully to participate in the life of God for the world.

As we noted at the beginning of this chapter, it is not our intention to present here a full account of spirituality. Adequate resources already exist elsewhere. It is appropriate, however, to focus briefly on three disciplines that seem to be of special significance for the work of compassion: prayer, reading the Bible, and worship.

The Reformers taught that petition was the highest form of prayer. In other words, in prayer we are ultimately concerned that God's will be done. God is the focus of prayer, not ourselves. That said, it is necessary to go on to say that if we are closed to God and to ourselves, God will surely have difficulty fulfilling the divine will in and through us. Inevitably, honest petition leads us to the most rigorous self-examination.

Each of us is enmeshed in the vicissitudes of human being: fear, anger, loneliness, pride, selfishness, anxiety, insecurity, pain, and so on. We are what Thomas Merton once called "a body of broken bones."[7] Time and again darkness threatens to engulf our lives. Desire and attachment fling us hither and yon, and we feel that our lives are like corks bobbing along on the top of tempestuous ocean waves. In other words, we can very easily find that we lack a center. We become strangers to ourselves and to one another. Our identities become uncertain. And the masks we wear increase in number, complexity, and depth day by day as we search earnestly for resources for survival.

Prayer always has a place in the work of returning to our true center, our being in Christ. In part, the discipline of prayer involves the struggle to identify and accept responsibility for the many and devious manifestations of the false self, the self that lives out of a center in itself rather than out of a center in Christ. What is referred to here as spiritual work is clearly self-knowledge. But more is implied, for it is self-knowledge in the context of who we are already in Jesus Christ. Alastair V. Campbell puts it well: "In order to care truly there is really no escape from the dread and pain of coming out of our hiding place into the full light of God's presence. We must learn to know our fears, our wounds, and our foolishness, and to know them in quite specific ways."[8]

Clearly this stringent work cannot be undertaken in a casual or careless way. It is a discipline that involves structures of silence and solitude in our lives by which we can

place ourselves before God. But prayer of this kind is not
without context or content to guide it. It is not free-floating introversion, colloquially called "navel gazing." True
prayer happens only in the context of the word of God, for
it is this word alone that leads us to a true knowledge of
ourselves. As Calvin noted, in well-known words: "It is
certain that man never achieves a clear knowledge of himself unless he has first looked upon God's face, and then
descends from contemplating him to scrutinize himself."[9]
It is surely close to the center of the Reformation traditions to insist that the Spirit works through the word to
which the Bible is the unique and authoritative witness.
Christian spirituality is biblical spirituality, a spirituality
which acknowledges that the Bible is a "guide and teacher
for anyone who would come to God."[10] This is precisely
the intention behind 2 Timothy 3:16–17; because it is inspired by God, scripture teaches the truth, refutes error,
and provides discipline for right living so that the person
of faith may be equipped to do God's work.

Eugene H. Peterson has given us the intriguing notion
of contemplative exegesis.[11] By this he means to draw our
attention to the fact that scripture is not a dead letter but
the living word of God. In contemplative exegesis we
allow the words of scripture to enter deeply into our beings, submitting our lives to the story that these words tell.
We allow the words and their story to shape us. The scripture affects us and changes us and opens us up to the
movement of God's Spirit. In this sense we have a dynamic
relationship with God through the scriptures that allows
us to plumb the depths of our human condition.

Christians through the centuries, and representing all
traditions, have prayed the psalms. This ancient collection
of prayers and songs can play a vital part in daily prayer,
enabling us to bring our deepest personal prayers to articulation. There is an honesty in the psalms, from the most
wrenching lament to the soaring heights of joy. A regular
discipline of praying the psalms allows us to travel deeper
and deeper into an open relationship with God that will

most certainly issue in profound self-knowledge. Fears, anxieties, and confusions as well as trust and confidence in God will all come to expression as we pray the psalms. We will less and less be able to hide from ourselves or continue to play the compulsive, furtive games that cripple our lives of faith. As both Israel and the church have recognized, the psalms are the artesian wells from which we obtain spiritual refreshment and new strength for the work of ministry. Praying the psalms grounds our faith and life in the most formative spirituality of the Judeo-Christian tradition, giving us rootedness and, thereby, the capacity to be nourished from the Source beyond ourselves.

Confession properly follows the reading of the Bible. Again, it is important to say that we know ourselves most fully in the light of God's word. It is as we read the Bible that we see ourselves in the searing light of God's redemption. Sin is understood reflectively in the light of God's forgiveness. We come to self-knowledge by finding ourselves in the stream of salvation history. The stories we read become our personal stories. We are the woman by the well, the tax collector, and the Pharisee. The exploration of sin and the naming of the masks we wear and the games we play is not a wallowing in self-pity or self-hatred. There has been a lot of misunderstanding about this. It is an honest look at ourselves in the light of the story, in the light of the fact that God loves us unconditionally, has elected us to be companions with God from the beginning of time, and in Jesus Christ has saved us from the dire consequences of our lies. Confession of sin is, in fact, a celebration of liberation whereby we move closer and closer to being in practice the persons God has redeemed us to be. It is a returning to our true center, our life in Jesus Christ.

Worship is the center of the church's and the Christian's life. Everything exists to praise God: work, prayer, recreation. To set worship apart from the whole of life is to stunt the understanding and practice of worship, turning it into an addendum to the real stuff of Monday-to-Friday living.

Worship becomes ecclesiastical entertainment or a religious balm to soothe battered souls. Christian spirituality,
if it would be true to its roots, is a spirituality that inevitably becomes communal and that sees worship as the central act from which everything else in faith and life takes
its reference.

Worship is an act of response to the will of God. It is the
act in which, above all else, we acknowledge that God is
the center of life. Worship is first of all something we do
in response to God and not something we experience for
ourselves. In worship there is a movement away from
ourselves to God. It is an act of obedience. For God com-
mands our worship, and without worship our relationship
with God remains sterile.

The word of God gives order to the worship of God: the
word read, preached, and celebrated. Worship happens in
the context of the fact that God has spoken. The preaching
of the word is not the giving of opinions. It is the announcement of God's word through the words of the preacher. It is
as the word is preached that one is able to find oneself
addressed by God. Baptism is the sacrament of the true self.
It reminds us again and again who we are because of whose
we are. We have identity in relationship with God through
God's act in Jesus Christ. Holy Communion is the sacrament of community, the sacrament that nurtures us in our
true selves. McNeill, Morrison, and Nouwen observe that
there is an intimate connection between compassion,
prayer, and the breaking of bread. This, they suggest, is
precisely what the description of the life of the early Christian community in Acts 2:42–47 tells us.[12] It is in Holy
Communion that we participate in Christ's life, which is
present for us in and through the elements. So participating in Christ's life we are nourished at the Lord's Table for
ministry, and that is why it is very hard to see how Christian
ministry is possible at all outside of the frequent celebration of the Holy Communion with the Lord.

Christianity cannot be nourished outside of word and
sacrament. They are the ground from which all else
springs. The spirituality of compassion must always be a

spirituality that has its roots deep in the worship life of the church.

Living with Our Woundedness

Lady Julian of Norwich, the fifteenth-century English mystic, prayed to God for three wounds: the wound of contrition, the wound of longing for God, and the wound of compassion.[13] As we have seen, to become compassionate is to be drawn into God's own woundedness. Julian understood that a circle of compassion, or woundedness, springs from the relations within the Trinity; it flows through Christ, is felt throughout creation, and, in those who love Christ, it returns again to God.[14] (To speak of compassion is to speak of woundedness, of a divine woundedness, first of all, but also of our human woundedness. Compassion means woundedness.)

The spirituality for compassion is a spirituality that must pay special attention to our woundedness. (It is sheer illusion to imagine that we can walk intimately with others in their woundedness if we have not been first of all intimately acquainted with our own woundedness) Education for compassion becomes education in our own woundedness.

Woundedness, of course, is not a new topic in the curriculum of ministry, although the consideration of woundedness is not usually seen to be a part of adult Christian education or of seminary preparation. Jesus certainly understood that following him would involve suffering for the disciple: "If any man would come after me, let him deny himself and take up his cross daily and follow me" (Luke 9:23). Again and again we read of Paul suffering with Christ, dying with Christ, and even completing in himself the sufferings of Christ. 2 Corinthians 1:3–4 is a text that anyone involved in ministry would do well to ponder:

> Blessed be the God and Father of our Lord Jesus
> Christ, the Father of mercies and God of all comfort,

who comforts us in all our affliction, so that we may be able to comfort those who are in any affliction, with the comfort with which we ourselves are comforted by God.

As Nouwen notes, "The great illusion of leadership is to think that man can be led out of the desert by someone who has never been there."[15] Later in the same epistle, at 12:9–10, Paul notes that his weakness is a virtue for ministry, for the Lord's power is at its best when he is weak. Not only did Paul make the connection between woundedness and ministry, he also understood that it was through his wounds, reminding him of his own weakness and therefore of his dependence upon God in all things, that ministry was possible in practical terms.

The relationship between woundedness, spirituality, and ministry has been memorably expressed in a quite remarkable passage in Chaim Potok's novel *The Chosen*. This is the story of two Jewish youths, one the son of a biblical scholar, the other the son of a Hasidic rabbi. The rabbi has brought up his son, Daniel, under a strict regime of study and silence. The book reaches its climax in a scene in the rabbi's study where the rabbi is speaking to his son through Rueven, Daniel's friend. The passage is worth citing at some length.

> When I was very young, my father, may he rest in peace, began to wake me in the middle of the night, just so I would cry. I was a child, but he would wake me and tell me stories of the destruction of Jerusalem and the sufferings of the people of Israel, and I would cry. . . . Once he took me to visit a hospital—ah, what an experience that was!—and often he took me to visit the poor, the beggars, to listen to them talk. My father himself never talked to me, except when we studied together. He taught me with silence. . . . When his people would ask him why he was so silent with his son, he would say to them that he did not like to talk, words are cruel, words play tricks, they distort what is in the heart, they conceal the heart, the heart speaks through silence. One learns of the pain of others by suffering

one's own pain, he would say, by turning inside oneself, by finding one's own soul. And it is important to know of pain, he said. It destroys our self-pride, our arrogance, our indifference toward others. It makes us aware of how frail and tiny we are and of how much we must depend upon the Master of the Universe. Only slowly, very slowly, did I begin to understand what he was saying. For years his silence bewildered and frightened me, although I always trusted him, I never hated him. And when I was old enough to understand, he told me that of all people a tzaddik especially must know of pain. A tzaddik must know how to suffer for his people, he said. He must take their pain from them and carry it on his own shoulders.[16]

The owning of woundedness in oneself is a particular part of the spirituality of compassion. As Chaim Potok has the rabbi say, "One learns of the pain of others by suffering one's own pain." This is a quite remarkable insight. Yet one of the hardest lessons for people to learn is that their woundedness, when it is named and owned, is often their most significant gift for ministry. Quite naturally, perhaps, we can imagine that we are called into ministry at the points of competency and control.

One evening, around dinnertime, I was called by the wife of one of my students. In obvious distress, she spoke of her husband's deep depression. Later that same evening, as I sat with them in the waiting room of a psychiatric clinic, my student expressed his conviction that his career in ministry was now abruptly over. His knowledge of himself as a deeply wounded person he saw as something that should bar him from ministry. The point is, however, that it is precisely our woundedness, when it has been uncovered and accepted for what it is, which allows us to be ministers, and which in particular makes compassion possible for us. If we are separated from our own woundedness, for whatever reason, compassion will in all likelihood become an impossibility for us.

It is important to know what is being claimed here. It is not enough simply to be wounded. Henri Nouwen

rightly notes that "open wounds stink and do not heal."[17]
We saw in the previous chapter, when we discussed Dorothee Soelle's work on apathy, that untreated wounds leave
us closed in on ourselves. Wounds left raw and sore lead
to the opposite of compassion; they lead to apathy. When
that happens we become strangers to our own personal
histories. (The fact that something hurts is not automati-
cally the prelude to compassion.)

Campbell notes quite correctly that "wounds, and the
vulnerability which they represent, lead to healing *only*
when they have been uncovered and dealt with; otherwise they are festering sores which destroy our health and
the health of those with whom we deal."[18] He goes on to
cite psychologist James Hillman: "I will be forced to pay
attention to my own sufferings and needs, if I am to be of
service to anyone else."[19] The wounded healer has to learn
to "speak" the language of his or her own woundedness
before trying to work with the woundedness of another.
One must have explored one's own experience of the valley of the shadow and found there the comfort and healing
of God before one can accompany another as he or she
walks through that valley.

(Neither is it enough to explore our own woundedness
solely as a psychological exercise.) It is terribly important
to understand that this work with woundedness is a dimension of life in Christ. We can return to Paul again to
get a theological perspective. He knew his woundedness;
he prayed on three occasions for healing, and he was told
that he would remain wounded. (But in and through the
weakness that his woundedness implied, God's grace was
sufficient and God's power was manifest, making ministry
possible (2 Cor. 12:9). Perhaps we can say that Paul discovered a sense of wholeness in which, although he remained
wounded, (his woundedness was experienced now in the
context of the grace and comfort of God.)

How do we name and own our woundedness in the
context of faith in Jesus Christ and begin through that
process to experience a new wholeness? The tradition of
the faith suggests two resources that are fundamental to

the process: lament and liturgy.[20] Lament is the language of crying out in which we struggle to articulate or at least express in some way the pain that is buried inside. Let us again return to the psalms. Walter Brueggemann notes that "serious religious use of the lament psalms has been minimal because we have believed that faith does not mean to acknowledge and embrace negativity. We have thought that acknowledgement of negativity was somehow an act of unfaith. . . . The point to be urged here is this: The use of these 'psalms of darkness' may be judged by the world to be *acts of unfaith and failure,* but for the trusting community, their use is *an act of bold faith.*" These psalms allow us to name what we really experience without covering awfulness up with pious rejection, as if true faith meant no negativity. They allow us to be honest with ourselves and honest with God. As Brueggemann notes, "These psalms make the important connection: everything must be *brought to speech,* and everything brought to speech must be *addressed to God.*"[21]

Bringing our woundedness to articulation through the reading of the psalms of lament allows for a kind of reality therapy. As Brueggemann says, language—in this case, the language of honest pain struggling to be expressed—leads experience (as if by a halter) so that which is unknown and unexperienced, that which is denied and hidden and repressed, may be brought to speech.[22] What was dimly felt but unnamed and unowned is given a language so that it may be brought into consciousness and awareness. Rather than providing the balm of a superficial and phony order, a kind of religious Walt Disney World, these psalms lead us to express what hitherto may have been felt to be inexpressible and was therefore denied, repressed, and buried. Certainly the outpourings may not be "proper"; some may find such blunt, raging religion to be offensive. But it is honest and biblical, and those who lament are seeking the healing and wholeness only God can provide.[23]

Our capacity for denial must not be underestimated. It is because woundedness is painful that we may do everything in our power to pretend to ourselves that we are not experiencing what we are experiencing. We cover up our deepest wounded feelings, and that gives us some sense of control, although it remains a lie. Fear, anxiety, and the threat of being overwhelmed are very powerful forces. From personal acquaintance we all know how we have denied suffering, from toothache to chest pain, from heartache to feelings of failure. We do not naturally come by the knowledge that the wounds must be cherished because, in a strange kind of way, they are a gift. But just as pain is a gift that alerts us to a malfunction in the body, so also woundedness is a gift that allows us to enter into the secret life of God. The fact that in our denial of suffering we remain distant from ourselves and from God should not be presumed to be sufficient incentive for us to come out of hiding. The fact too that the psalms of lament are rarely used in our churches should not be a surprise to us.

Liturgy means the work of the people. It is the worship equivalent of the great Reformation principle of the priesthood of all believers (the worship participation of all believers!). Through the dramas of the liturgies the faith comes to worshipful expression as the vocation of all Christians. As liturgy, worship has form; but the form of the liturgy is not an end in itself.[24] It points away from itself, so to speak, to the one whom it serves, Jesus Christ, the Lord of the church. Liturgy ensures that no one is excluded from active participation in the worship of God through the Son.

Worship as liturgy is not a passive act centered on the worship leader, who controls everything by having complete authority over what words are said and what tone is set. It is somewhat ironic that many Protestants are afraid of liturgy for fear of Romanizing worship, yet the pulpit-centered worship so dearly defended has become nothing less than a homiletical sacerdotalism before which the people remain passive recipients. It is priestcraft of another order, and priestcraft just the same.

Worship as liturgy is the work of the people in which the drama of redemption is rehearsed in such a way that the people, individually and corporately, can find their place in that drama so it becomes also their story. Liturgy brings life into worship and worship to life. The human story finds its place in God's story. Liturgy, as it gives careful attention to the church year and the lectionary, allows each of us to find the place of our joys and pains, the place of our moments of ecstasy, and the place of our moments of terror, in the stream of salvation history. Liturgy, in its sensitivity to tradition, reminds us that we are not the first pilgrims to pass this way with these experiences. Our prayers join in the prayers of the whole church, past and present, on earth and in heaven, as we know so well from the great doxology:

> Praise God from whom all blessings flow;
> Praise God, all creatures here below;
> Praise God above, ye heavenly host:
> Praise Father, Son, and Holy Ghost.

Just as the psalms allow us to express our deepest experiences in one medium, liturgy allows expression in another medium, in which senses and emotions, symbols and ideas enable us to gather all of life together, the good parts as well as the bad parts, in the shared act of worship. The lament and the liturgy combine to enable us to express the inexpressible in the context of prayer and worship. The heart of the work of naming and owning our woundedness is not solely the psychological process of coming into self-awareness, important as that is. It is, rather, the process of discovering oneself, and one's experiences of suffering, through one's participation in the ancient language and rituals of faith, in the psalms of lament and in liturgy.

(Spirituality and compassion come together in a practical way when we learn to speak the language of woundedness. If we cannot "speak" (perhaps we should say "shout") this language, if we have not entered into the mystery and power of our own wounds, compassion will always slip away from us.)

Naming woundedness is difficult work. In fact, left to ourselves it is probably an impossible task. It would be foolish and naïve to pretend otherwise. However, we are not asked to make the journey alone. Just as we in compassion can walk with others through their dark night of suffering and be a part of the process of their coming into the light of healing by being a companion, so also we need the compassionate community to be a companion to us so that we too can come into our healing. We all need persons who will not be too quick to take our pain away but who will have the spiritual and mental toughness to walk with us, sharing in our journey to the point where woundedness can be confronted at its source. Shared woundedness, says Nouwen, becomes mobilizing.[25] The sting is drawn because the secret is shared. Community emerges as the fruit of intimacy. "A Christian community is therefore a healing community not because wounds are cured and pains are alleviated, but because wounds and pains become openings or occasions for a new vision."[26]

Spirituality, woundedness, and compassion are bound together. Each implies the others. Compassion comes to birth through us when we recognize this. We are cast back upon God in Christ, who alone can carry our woundedness as well as the woundedness of the world. And in a way that is quite countercultural, we recognize that true authority for ministry, the authority of compassion,[27] is found in the power of our wounds.

Compassion and Interdependency: Being the Church

These reflections on spirituality, woundedness, and compassion lead us to see that the spirituality for compassion becomes a spirituality of interdependency, a spirituality of community. On the day of his death Thomas Merton said that "the whole idea of compassion . . . is based on a keen awareness of the interdependence of all these living beings, which are all part of one another and all involved in one another."[28] Here he repeated what he had said most eloquently elsewhere. Writing of his life as a Trappist monk from the hindsight of twenty years in the monastery, he remarked that "my monastery . . . is a place in which I disappear from the world as an object of interest in order to be everywhere in it by hiddenness and compassion."[29] Interdependence: being everywhere connected in hiddenness and compassion—this is an astonishingly sublime vision of the Christian life.

In a similar way, Matthew Fox recognizes that compassion is about interdependence. "Compassion," he suggests, "is a healing by way of making connections."[30] As he develops his theme, compassion is the happy marriage of mysticism and social justice, the seeing and the making of connections. In other words, compassion is a way of being a person that has its hidden ground in the internal relations within the Holy Trinity and its outer expression in ministry.

Interdependence is not just another way of saying the obvious: namely, that we are social beings. What we speak of is found already in Paul's vision of the church as the body of Christ (1 Cor. 6:15; 10:17; 12:12–13f.; Rom. 12:4–5; Eph. 4:4–6, 25; Col. 3:11, 15; Gal. 3:28). In fact, the evocative image of the church as a body only makes sense in terms of interdependence. At 1 Corinthians 12:14–21, for example, Paul gives ample illustration of the interconnectedness of the parts of the body. Interestingly, for our purposes, he goes on, at verse 26, to say that if one part of the body is hurt, all parts hurt with it. Being the body, being the church, involves interdependency and the sharing of woundedness. Certainly this stands over against our privatized notions of being the church, in which we imagine that we each belong to Christ individually and without mutual responsibility.

Interdependence and shared woundedness define us as the body of Christ. Compassion is part of the fabric of ecclesiology, part of the weave of the church. This should not surprise us, in view of all that has gone before. Because Jesus Christ is the compassionate Lord, his body is necessarily the compassionate community. And just as compassion marks the church's being as church, likewise there can be no compassion outside of the interdependent relationships which form community. The spirituality for compassion is a spirituality of the body, a spirituality that builds

up the church according to its true nature, which lies
hidden in Christ, thereby enabling it to become increasingly in practice the compassionate presence of its compassionate Lord.

The spirituality of compassion is not, in the last analysis,
a private spirituality. Compassion is a social reality. It calls
for a spirituality of community in which worship and
prayer, study and ministry, encouragement and account-
ability bind us together. And at its center, surely, is the
celebration of the Holy Communion, the sacrament of
community that reminds us of our utter dependence upon
God. The community gathers together to receive the living Word and be formed again in union with Jesus Christ,
the incarnation of the compassion of God.

6

The Practice of Compassion: Concluding Reflections on Ministry

The task of pastoral theology is primarily theological, being that part of Christian dogmatics in which we think through the meaning of the gospel in terms of the ministry of the church—an eminently practical task, it should be added. The pastoral theologian has a particular vocation to make connections with the actual work of ministry in the day-to-day lives of the people of the church. That connection must always be made explicit.[1]

It should be clear by now that we cannot write a manual for compassion. Compassion is not a technical skill to be mastered. It is really a form of theological existence, of living into Christ. Nevertheless, compassion in practice does have definite form. We would be amiss were we not now to press on and suggest briefly something of the shape of compassionate ministry. What does compassionate ministry look like?

In a very real sense, this question has been answered already; everything discussed up to this point has addressed it. Yet it is still appropriate to keep pressing the question, and to insist that the foregoing be pulled together into a concluding vision of ministry.

First of all, it is important to reassert the primary fact about compassion: Compassion means ministry. It is not a sentimental feeling sorry for someone. As we found it uniquely demonstrated in the life of Jesus, compassion is an action word, a verb. In compassion the person in need

is addressed by the gospel in specific ways. This characterizes compassion, distinguishing it from pity, sympathy,
mercy, and empathy.

Second, compassion is a hands-on ministry. This, we discovered, does not mean that compassion is only a ministry
of touching, although it has a significant place for touching. The image conveys, rather, something of the degree
of intimacy, solidarity, and immediacy involved in compassion. Compassion is not caring from a distance. It has
a face-to-face quality, and something of the sense of presence and involvement. It is a ministry of making connections. In the best sense of the word, we might call it a
ministry of relationship. It is a ministry of being a traveling
companion. In compassion we walk with others through
their suffering, shepherding them by entering with them
into the mystery of their suffering.

Third, compassion is a ministry that breaks through the
barriers of social and religious convention. It is a ministry
without limits, leading beyond what some persons may
regard as an acceptable level of commitment. It can demand great personal cost. Although in popular culture
compassion is sometimes taken to be a wimpish emotion,
we have discovered that it is tough-minded ministry. In
compassionate ministry one is obedient to love's demand
to go the second mile. Compassion demands persistence
even when prudence would suggest otherwise.

The "foolishness" of compassion, the fact that it leads us
beyond the pale, is illustrated by a story from the medieval
church concerning St. Martin of Tours. The story comes
from a book by David Adam, *The Cry of the Deer,* which
is a series of meditations on the hymn of St. Patrick.

> Whilst still in the army and preparing to become a
> Christian, Martin was stationed near Amiens. One cold
> day, he went out with his soldier companions. They
> wore heavy cloaks to protect them from the bitter
> weather. Their cloaks were among their prized posses-
> sions. As they approached the city gates, they met a
> beggar who was near naked and about to perish with

the cold. As soon as he saw him, Martin was moved with compassion. He drew his sword and cut his cloak in two, giving one part to the beggar. His companions jeered and mocked him for his foolishness; they would not let him forget such folly in a hurry. That night Martin had a vision. He saw into the kingdom of heaven, and there was Christ surrounded by angels. Christ was wearing the cloak that Martin had given to the beggar. Martin heard Christ say, "Look, this is the cloak which Martin has given to me this day." Martin had discovered the great secret of God Incarnate.[2]

This rather strange tale shows how caring in compassion goes beyond limits. There is a sense in which it makes no sense. It is not cost-effective. It does not respond satisfactorily to the administration of goals and strategies, so fondly embraced today by church administrators. In compassion we may march to the beat of a fairly noninstitutional drummer. That can make compassion dangerous. We may catch a whiff of anarchy as we draw near to compassion. And yet, as we see time and again in the history of the church, this is precisely what ministry to the marginalized persons will often demand of us.

Fourth, compassion is an evangelical ministry. The notion of evangelicalism is something of a religious red flag, of course. It can be a badge of orthodoxy or carry theological associations that mark it as unacceptably conservative. Yet the fundamental image of evangelicalism, that of bringing persons to Christ where they may "taste and see that the Lord is good" and so arrive at their own decisions in the matter of faith, is, without a doubt, integral to the life of the church. It is hard to conceive of a Christian church that would not want to spread the good news of God's compassion in Jesus Christ.

Compassion does not call for an ecclesiastical welfare state, a ministry that induces quietism and dependency. Neither is it cheap grace. Compassion is the ministry of Jesus Christ by which he personally enters into another's brokenness. By thus entering a person's life, Christ in compassion calls for faith and discipleship. In the fullest sense our healing and wholeness can only come when we have entered into a relationship with the one who is the source of compassion, Jesus Christ.

Fifth, compassion is a situational ministry. This does not mean, of course, that it has no structure or form. Compassion is not free-floating, undisciplined caring. The image of situationalism is intended to convey the idea that compassion cannot be prepackaged or arranged somehow in advance to cover all imaginable eventualities. Compassionate responses are tailor-made to the situation, as Jesus Christ responds to us uniquely and personally. They are the mediation of the gospel, in all of its particularity, for each event and every person. Compassion is a situational—that is, relational—ministry in which each response is marked with novelty and uniqueness.

Sixth, compassion is a vicarious ministry. Usually defined as "suffering with" another, we discovered that compassion can sometimes be stretched in meaning to become a "suffering for" another. It is the ministry of the father who bore his prodigal son's sin; it is Christ's ministry of atonement when he died for the sin of the world. As a vicarious ministry it is a priestly ministry, in which the suffering of another is borne in order to be borne away. Of all the aspects of compassion this vicarious dimension perhaps is the most difficult to understand and to enter into because it is supremely and uniquely the ministry of Jesus Christ.

As we participate in Christ's compassion more and more fully, we might well expect that we would be called to participate in its priestly aspect. Vicarious compassion becomes the expression of our intimacy with Christ in the deepest sense. As the saints knew well, intimacy with God always leads to deeper suffering. And this is what we find with compassion. Vicarious compassion is a redemptive ministry in which we find our lives giving expression to the mystery and love at the heart of the gospel.

Examples of the vicarious dimension of compassion are elusive because in many ways it is a secret ministry, hidden from public view. A parent suffers for a child, a teacher for a student, one friend for another. It is a ministry of pain borne and tears shed in order that another may carry a lighter burden. It is a ministry of forgiveness in order that another may come to repentance. It is a ministry of reconciliation in order that community may be formed.

Seventh, compassion is a ministry that bridges the gap between social and pastoral ministries. For far too long we have had to work with outmoded and stereotypical assumptions about ministries of social action and ministries of pastoral care. We assumed that there was little interconnection. But the plain truth is, there is a problem in our core conception of ministry if we feel that we must choose between a social and a pastoral ministry. Such exclusivism opens up a vicious dualism, causing ministry to become one-sided and fractured. Compassion is neither a social nor a pastoral ministry only, neither exclusively ministry to society or large groups nor ministry to individuals. In the New Testament, as we saw, Jesus ministered in compassion to social needs and to pastoral needs. It is the whole person who is the focus of compassion, and at the end of the day that is always the person in community and the person in relationships. Here in the compassionate community we see the common goal of both social and pastoral ministry: the service of the kingdom of God.

Walter Brueggemann comments that in compassion Jesus brings together the internalization of pain and external transformation. The fact that Jesus weeps, that he has compassion, contrasts with the dominant culture. Jesus dismantles the power of death by submitting himself to the pain and grief present in the situation.

> The compassion of Jesus is to be understood not simply as a personal emotional reaction but as a public criticism in which he dares to act upon his concern against the entire numbness of his social context. . . . Thus compassion that might be seen simply as generous goodwill is in fact criticism of the system, forces, and

ideologies that produce the hurt. Jesus enters into the
hurt and finally comes to embody it.[3]

Compassion is both pastoral and social ministry.

Further, we must go on to say that in compassion Jesus
also had nothing to do with any kind of dualism between
the spirit and the body. Compassionate ministry has nothing to do with either flights from bodiliness or flights from
spirituality. It is always the whole person who is attended
to in compassionate ministry, the person who feels, eats,
gets sick, and is or is not in a right relationship with God.
We can sum up what we intend here in an aphorism:

> Prayer without compassion leads to piety;
> compassion without prayer leads to pity.

Social justice, pastoral care, and spiritual formation belong
together as the interconnected foci of compassionate ministry.

Eight, it must be emphasized (it cannot be overempha-
sized!) how important spirituality is to compassionate ministry. Because our compassion is a participation in Jesus'
compassion, in which we enter into the inner life of the
Holy Trinity, there can be no possibility of compassion
outside of relationship with Jesus Christ. Relationship with
Jesus Christ is *the* necessary condition from our side that
makes compassion possible for us. Growth in compassion
is the fruit of our life in Christ.

At its heart, the language of compassion is the language
of spirituality and theology rather than the language of
social work and psychotherapy. The saint, if we may speak
this way, rather than the professional is what is called for.
"Before any professional skill," says Nouwen, "we need a
spirituality, a way of living in the spirit."[4] Increasingly,
however, ministries of caring have been described almost
solely in terms of technical and professional skills, with
little reference to relationship with Christ. In what he calls
"the professional captivity of pastoral care," Alastair V.
Campbell notes that "expertise is equated with excel-
lence; and it is assumed that there is a straightforward

connection between professional counseling and Christian caring."[5] When caring is seen from the perspective of professional counseling, the lay person is virtually excluded from participation in pastoral care and we have to invent something called "lay pastoral care" to find a job for the nonclergy to do. It is not at all clear what the theological basis for such a dualistic view of caring ministry might be. The ministry of compassion is a ministry into which all Christians are called by virtue of their faith in Jesus Christ.

Of course there can be no tolerance of incompetency in ministry. Let there be no doubt about that. But skill is not at the center of compassion. Rather, skill is to be seen as the servant of theology and spirituality.

Ninth, and finally, although compassion is not the complete gospel, it is appropriate to recall that the evangelist Matthew used compassion to sum up Jesus' ministry at one point. Although there was more to Jesus' life and ministry than compassion, it is incontrovertibly true that there can be no adequate account of his life and ministry or of the church's ministry that does not give compassion its rightful place. While we cannot collapse theology and ministry into compassion without massive and damaging reductionism, neither can we continue to neglect compassion without an equally damaging reductionism. Compassion has been a forgotten topic in Christian pastoral theology and ministry. It is necessary to place it back now onto center stage.[6] It has been our intent to play a part in rescuing compassion from neglect and to put it back into the language and practice of ministry. It is in the search for a renewed compassion that both clergy and laity can find a profound rootedness in the life of God and participate in God's continuing work of redeeming the world. Compassion is nothing less than a form of theological existence in which we participate in Christ's ministry to the Father, in the power of the Holy Spirit, for the sake of the world.

Notes

Introduction: The Search for a Renewed Compassion

1. Nicholas Wolterstorff, *Lament for a Son* (Grand Rapids: Wm. B. Eerdmans Publishing Co., 1987), p. 34.
2. See Kenneth Leech, *Spirituality and Pastoral Care* (London: Sheldon Press, 1986), pp. 5–6.
3. Karl Barth, *Church Dogmatics* III/2 (Edinburgh: T. & T. Clark, 1960), p. 211.

Chapter 1: Compassion in the Ministry of Jesus

1. This story was told to me. I have been unable to verify if it is indeed a genuine *Peanuts* cartoon.
2. Compassion is used as a noun at Luke 1:78. Compassion is also found occasionally in the New Testament letters. Paul, for example, uses the noun form to refer to the total human personality at the deepest level. For a review see Helmut Köster, *"Splanchnon,"* Gerhard Friedrich, ed., *Theological Dictionary of the New Testament*, vol. 7 (Grand Rapids: Wm. B. Eerdmans Publishing Co., 1971), pp. 555–556.
3. This is a disputed use of compassion. Many commentators— Lane, Cranfield, Taylor, Manson, Anderson, for example—argue that v. 41 should read *orgistheis*, moved to anger, rather than *splanchnistheis*, moved with compassion, as the preferred reading. Bruce M. Metzger argues the contrary position in *A Textual Commentary on the Greek New Testament* (London: United Bible Societies, 1975), p. 76. A full discussion is available in William L. Lane, *The Gospel According to Mark* (Grand Rap-

ids: Wm. B. Eerdmans Publishing Co., 1974), p. 84, note 141.
4. Lane, *Mark*, p. 87.
5. Thomas Merton, *The Asian Journal of Thomas Merton* (New York: New Directions Publishing Corp., 1973), pp. 341–342.
6. Jesus' compassion has to be read back here. There is no reason to suppose that his response was anything less than compassionate, however. The parallel text at Matthew 17:15 has the father plead for mercy. The parallel text at Luke 9:37–43 has no mention of mercy or compassion.
7. Dietrich Bonhoeffer, *The Cost of Discipleship*, tr. R. H. Fuller (London: SCM Press, 1959), p. 37.
8. Some commentators separate Mark 6:30–34 from 6:35–44. See Lane, *Mark*, pp. 224–227, for a review of the arguments. Ulrich Mauser remarks that "Mark has unmistakably established a connexion between the disciples' journey and the feeding of the five thousand by his transitional remarks in 6:30–34. Here the wilderness theme is obvious." See *Christ in the Wilderness* (Naperville, Ill.: Alec R. Allenson, 1963), p. 134.
9. Mauser, *Christ in the Wilderness*.
10. Ibid., p. 135.
11. Ibid.
12. Lane, *Mark*, p. 273.
13. See Robert H. Gundry, *Matthew: A Commentary on His Literary and Theological Art* (Grand Rapids: Wm. B. Eerdmans Publishing Co., 1982), pp. 289–290, for details.
14. Eugene H. Peterson, *Five Smooth Stones for Pastoral Work* (Atlanta: John Knox Press, 1980), p. 14.
15. For discussion see Lane, *Mark*, pp. 271–272.
16. Seward Hiltner, *Preface to Pastoral Theology* (Nashville: Abingdon Press, 1958), p. 68.
17. Gundry, *Matthew*, p. 406.
18. Donald P. McNeill, Douglas A. Morrison, and Henri J. M. Nouwen, *Compassion: A Reflection on the Christian Life* (Garden City, N.Y.: Doubleday & Co., 1982), p. 4.
19. Ibid., p. 27.
20. Helmut Köster notes that in each case of the use of compassion in synoptic narratives we have "a Messianic characterization of Jesus rather than the mere depiction of an emotion. All these interjections are thus part of the tendency of the tradition to describe Jesus increasingly in terms of Messianic attributes. The same applies to the one instance in Luke . . . i.e., the young man at Nain." Köster, *"Splanchnon,"* loc. cit., p. 555.

21. Gundry, *Matthew*, p. 180.
22. Martin Buber, *Between Man and Man*, tr. Ronald Gregor Smith (Macmillan Co., 1965), p. 13. I found this illustration in Douglas Steere, *Together in Solitude* (New York: Crossroad Publishing Co., 1982), p. 165.
23. McNeill, Morrison, and Nouwen, *Compassion*, p. 92.
24. Simone Weil, *Waiting for God* (Glasgow: Wm. Collins Sons & Co., 1983), p. 75.

Chapter 2: Compassion in the Teaching of Jesus

1. Joachim Jeremias, *The Parables of Jesus* (London: SCM Press, 1972), p. 12.
2. Köster, loc. cit., ch. 1, note 2, p. 554.
3. Ibid., p. 553.
4. Jürgen Moltmann, *Theology of Hope*, tr. James W. Leitch (London: SCM Press, 1967), p. 21. Readers familiar with Moltmann's early work on eschatology will detect its influence on this discussion.
5. Kenneth E. Bailey, *Through Peasant Eyes* (Grand Rapids: Wm. B. Eerdmans Publishing Co., 1980), pp. 34–35. The subsequent discussion is much indebted to Bailey's work.
6. Ibid., p. 43.
7. Ibid., p. 48.
8. Jeremias, *Parables*, p. 204.
9. Bailey, *Through Peasant Eyes*, p. 46.
10. Ibid., p. 49.
11. Ibid., p. 52.
12. Ibid., p. 54.
13. Ibid., p. 55.
14. Jeremias, *Parables*, p. 205.
15. Bailey, *Through Peasant Eyes*, p. 54.
16. Kenneth E. Bailey, *Poet and Peasant* (Grand Rapids: Wm. B. Eerdmans Publishing Co., 1976), p. 206.
17. See Bailey, *Poet and Peasant*, pp. 205–206. This interpretation of the parable is a loose paraphrase of Bailey's masterful summary.
18. Kenneth E. Bailey, "A Draft of Through Peasant Eyes," the manuscript of a preseminary course, Assuit College, Assuit, Egypt. The copy is located in the library of Pittsburgh Theological Seminary. There is no date. The citation is from p. 18.
19. Bailey, *Poet and Peasant*, p. 181.

20. Ibid., pp. 181–182.
21. Bailey, "A Draft of Through Peasant Eyes," p. 23.
22. Jeremias, *Parables,* p. 132.
23. Bailey, *Poet and Peasant,* p. 190.
24. Ibid., p. 203.
25. See Matthew Fox, *A Spirituality Named Compassion and the Healing of the Global Village, Humpty Dumpty and Us* (Minneapolis: Winston Press, 1979), pp. 2–3.

Chapter 3: A Theology of Divine Compassion

1. J. K. Mozley, *The Impassibility of God* (Cambridge: Cambridge University Press, 1926), p. 127.
2. Jürgen Moltmann, *The Crucified God,* tr. R. A. Wilson and John Bowden (New York: Harper & Row, 1974), p. 267. See also G. L. Prestige, *God in Patristic Thought* (London: S.P.C.K., 1952), pp. 11–12, and Eberhard Jüngel, *God as the Mystery of the World,* tr. Darrell L. Guder (Grand Rapids: Wm. B. Eerdmans Publishing Co., 1983), pp. 39–40.
3. Moltmann, *The Crucified God,* p. 268.
4. Cited in Mozley, *Impassibility of God,* p. 112.
5. Walter Brueggemann, Editor's Foreword to Terence E. Fretheim, *The Suffering of God: An Old Testament Perspective* (Philadelphia: Fortress Press, 1984), p. xii.
6. See Jürgen Moltmann, *The Trinity and the Kingdom: The Doctrine of God* (San Francisco: Harper & Row, 1982), p. 25.
7. Abraham J. Heschel, *The Prophets: An Introduction* (New York: Harper & Row, 1962), p. 24.
8. Ibid., p. 219.
9. Cited in Mozley, *Impassibility of God,* p. 104.
10. Moltmann, *The Crucified God,* p. 270.
11. Fretheim, *The Suffering of God,* p. 108.
12. Ibid., p. 109.
13. Ibid., p. 111.
14. Ibid.
15. Ibid., p. 112.
16. Ibid., p. 116.
17. Ibid., p. 121.
18. Ibid., p. 133.
19. Ibid., p. 135.
20. Ibid., p. 137.
21. Ibid., pp. 140–143.

22. Samuel H. Dresner, *Prayer, Humility, and Compassion* (Philadelphia: Jewish Publication Society of America, 1957), p. 239. Every effort has been made to avoid the use of pronouns for God. The insertion of a pronoun here is necessary, I believe, in order to convey a profoundly intimate and personal reference to God which pronoun-free language is apt to miss.

23. Ibid., p. 193.

24. Ibid., p. 219.

25. Moltmann, *The Trinity and the Kingdom*, p. 165.

26. Thomas F. Torrance, *Divine and Contingent Order* (Oxford: Oxford University Press, 1981), p. 7.

27. Thomas F. Torrance, *Space, Time and Incarnation* (London: Oxford University Press, 1969), p. 75.

28. Jüngel, *God as the Mystery of the World*, p. 39.

29. Ibid., p. 13.

30. See Moltmann, *The Crucified God*, p. 241.

31. Ibid., p. 243.

32. Ibid., p. 4.

33. Köster, loc. cit., ch. 1, note 2, p. 553.

34. This is the question which the late Patristic doctrine of *perichoresis* tried to address. See Prestige, *God in Patristic Thought*, pp. 291–292.

35. Moltmann, *The Trinity and the Kingdom*, p. 27.

36. Cited in Mozley, *Impassibility of God*, p. 140.

37. Ray S. Anderson, "A Theology for Ministry," in Ray S. Anderson, ed., *Theological Foundations for Ministry* (Grand Rapids: Wm. B. Eerdmans Publishing Co., 1979), pp. 9 and 20.

38. Karl Barth, *Church Dogmatics* III/2 (Edinburgh: T. & T. Clark, 1960), p. 211.

39. Elie Wiesel, *Night*, tr. Stella Rodway (Hammondsworth, England: Penguin Books, 1960), pp. 76–77.

Chapter 4: A Theology of Compassionate Suffering

1. Arthur C. McGill, *Suffering: A Test of Theological Method* (Philadelphia: Westminster Press, 1982), p. 34.

2. Donald P. McNeill, Douglas A. Morrison, and Henri J. M. Nouwen, *Compassion: A Reflection on the Christian Life* (Garden City, N.Y.: Doubleday & Co., 1982), p. 8.

3. Kazoh Kitamori, *Theology of the Pain of God* (Richmond: John Knox Press, 1965), p. 86.

4. See Rollo May, *Love and Will* (New York: W. W. Norton & Co., 1969), ch. 1.

5. See R. J. Lipton, "Apathy and Numbness—A Modern Temptation" in Flavian Dougherty, ed., *The Meaning of Human Suffering* (New York: Human Sciences Press, 1982), pp. 196–197.

6. See May, *Love and Will.*

7. Dorothee Soelle, *Suffering,* tr. Everett R. Kalin (Philadelphia: Fortress Press, 1975), p. 36.

8. Ibid., p. 40.

9. Ibid., p. 38.

10. Walter Brueggemann, *The Prophetic Imagination* (Philadelphia: Fortress Press, 1978), p. 42.

11. Ibid., p. 46.

12. For a discussion see my article, "Cancer and Official Theology," *The Christian Century,* Sept. 11–18, 1985.

13. Soelle, *Suffering,* p. 69.

14. Ibid., p. 73.

15. Ibid., p. 70.

16. Eugene H. Peterson, *Five Smooth Stones for Pastoral Work* (Atlanta: John Knox Press, 1980), p. 114.

17. Henri J. M. Nouwen, *The Wounded Healer* (Garden City, N.Y.: Doubleday & Co., Image Books, 1979), p. 92.

18. Soelle, *Suffering,* p. 74.

19. John le Carré, *Tinker, Tailor, Soldier, Spy* (New York: Bantam Books, 1975), p. 203.

20. See John Biersdorf, *Healing of Purpose* (Nashville: Abingdon Press, 1985), who discusses this proposition.

21. See Ray S. Anderson, "A Theology for Ministry," in Ray S. Anderson, ed., *Theological Foundations for Ministry* (Grand Rapids: Wm. B. Eerdmans Publishing Co., 1979).

22. These general remarks and the discussion following are indebted to a study of suffering in the Bible by Erhard S. Gerstenberger and Wolfgang Schrage, *Suffering,* tr. John E. Steely (Nashville: Abingdon Press, 1980).

23. Ibid., pp. 103–104, for a discussion of these themes in detail.

24. Ibid., p. 147.

25. For an extended discussion of this point see Jürgen Moltmann, *Theology of Hope* (London: SCM Press, 1957), ch. 5, and Brueggemann, *The Prophetic Imagination,* pp. 85–86.

26. The following presentation is indebted to Robert C. Tannehill's detailed study *Dying and Rising with Christ: A Study*

in *Pauline Theology* (Berlin: Verlag Alfred Töpelmann, 1967).
27. Ibid., p. 84.
28. Ibid., p. 85.
29. Ibid., p. 86.
30. Ibid., p. 87.
31. Ibid., p. 90.

Chapter 5: Living with the Wound of Compassion

1. For a critical discussion of climbing Jacob's ladder see Matthew Fox, *A Spirituality Named Compassion and the Healing of the Global Village, Humpty Dumpty and Us* (Minneapolis: Winston Press, 1979), pp. 36–37.
2. Thomas Merton, *New Seeds of Contemplation* (New York: New Directions, 1961), pp. 31–32.
3. The image is from Merton, but see Donald P. McNeill, Douglas A. Morrison, and Henri J. M. Nouwen, *Compassion: A Reflection on the Christian Life* (Garden City, N.Y.: Doubleday & Co., 1982), pp. 66–67.
4. Merton, *New Seeds of Contemplation,* p. 37.
5. McNeill, Morrison, and Nouwen, *Compassion,* p. 90.
6. Ibid., p. 91.
7. Merton, *New Seeds of Contemplation,* pp. 70–71.
8. Alastair V. Campbell, *Rediscovering Pastoral Care* (Philadelphia: Westminster Press, 1981), p. 106.
9. John Calvin, *Institutes of the Christian Religion,* ed. J. T. McNeill and tr. Ford Lewis Battles, The Library of Christian Classics, vol. 20 (Philadelphia: Westminster Press, 1960), 1.1.2, p. 37.
10. Ibid., 1.6.1, p. 69.
11. Eugene H. Peterson, *Working the Angles: The Shape of Pastoral Integrity* (Grand Rapids: Wm. B. Eerdmans Publishing Co., 1987), pp. 74–75.
12. McNeill, Morrison, and Nouwen, *Compassion,* p. 112.
13. Julian of Norwich, *Showings* (New York: Paulist Press, 1978), p. 127.
14. For a discussion see Julia Gatta, *Three Spiritual Directors for Our Time: Julian of Norwich, the Cloud of Unknowing, Walter Hilton* (Cambridge, Mass.: Cowley Publications, 1987).
15. Henri J. M. Nouwen, *The Wounded Healer* (Garden City, N.Y.: Doubleday & Co., Image Books, 1979), p. 72.

16. Chaim Potok, *The Chosen* (New York: Simon & Schuster, 1967), p. 278. A tzaddik is a righteous man.
17. Nouwen, *The Wounded Healer*, p. 88.
18. Campbell, *Rediscovering Pastoral Care*, pp. 49–50.
19. Ibid., p. 50.
20. See Dorothee Soelle, *Suffering*, tr. Everett R. Kalin (Philadelphia: Fortress Press, 1975), p. 72.
21. Walter Brueggemann, *The Message of the Psalms* (Minneapolis: Augsburg Publishing House, 1984), p. 52. It is interesting that Brueggemann goes on to note that it is more appropriate to refer to this God who wills our honesty in the categories of fidelity rather than immutability.
22. Ibid., p. 53.
23. The psalms of lament are 3, 4, 5, 7, 10, 17, 22, 25, 26, 28, 31, 39, 42, 43, 54, 55, 56, 57, 59, 61, 64, 69, 70, 71, 77, 120, 140, 141, 142. Brueggemann also lists seven penitential psalms: 6, 32, 38, 51, 102, 130, 143 (ibid., p. 187).
24. J. J. von Allmen, *Worship: Its Theology and Practice*, tr. Harold Knight and W. Fletcher Fleet (London: Lutterworth Press, 1965), pp. 80–81.
25. Nouwen, *The Wounded Healer*, p. 93.
26. Ibid., p. 94.
27. Nouwen uses this image, ibid., p. 41.
28. Thomas Merton, *The Asian Journal of Thomas Merton* (New York: New Directions Publishing Corp., 1973), pp. 341–342.
29. Thomas Merton, Preface to the Japanese edition, *The Seven Storey Mountain* (Tokyo: Toyo Publishing Co., 1965). This citation is found in McNeill, Morrison, and Nouwen, *Compassion*, p. 143.
30. Fox, *A Spirituality Named Compassion*, p. iii.

Chapter 6: The Practice of Compassion

1. Sometimes the making of connections involves the work of what has come to be called practical theology. This is not some kind of applied theology, as if theology in itself were somehow impractical. Rather, practical theology is the work of engaging in dialogue with knowledge from other disciplines concerned with human welfare in order that ministry may be fully and responsibly informed.

2. David Adam, *The Cry of the Deer* (London: Triangle/ S.P.C.K., 1987), pp. 24–25.

3. Walter Brueggemann, *The Prophetic Imagination* (Philadelphia: Fortress Press, 1978), pp. 85–86.

4. Henri J. M. Nouwen, *The Living Reminder* (New York: Seabury Press, 1981), p. 28.

5. Alastair V. Campbell, *Professionalism and Pastoral Care* (Philadelphia: Fortress Press, 1985), p. 45.

6. It was with some sadness that I discovered a major recent publication in pastoral care, representing contributions from leading thinkers in the field, carried no entry under compassion. See Alastair V. Campbell, ed., *A Dictionary of Pastoral Care* (London: S.P.C.K., 1987).

Printed in the United States
66457LVS00002B/19-36